Who's At Home In Your Body (When You're Not)?

Essays on Consciousness by a Participant Observer

Also by Stephen Rich Merriman, Ph.D:

When You Lose What You Can't Live Without

Outside Time: My Friendship with Wilbur

The Living Oracle: Wisdom & Divination for Everyday Life

Pathfinding Through Multiple Personality

Anger and Rage Addiction & the Self-Pact

Who's At Home In Your Body (When You're Not)?

**Essays on Consciousness
by a Participant Observer**

Stephen Rich Merriman

Four Rivers Press

San Francisco, California
Amherst, Massachusetts
www.fourriverspress.com

WHO'S AT HOME IN YOUR BODY
(WHEN YOU'RE NOT)?
ESSAYS ON CONSCIOUSNESS
BY A PARTICIPANT OBSERVER

Published by Four Rivers Press

All rights reserved
Copyright @ 2010 by Stephen Rich Merriman

Cover art by Emily Sara Taylor Merriman.
Used by permission of the artist.

Book design by Tim Kinnel, www.wordsareimages.com

Permission is granted to copy, quote or reprint portions
of this book for purposes of review; for all other uses, please contact
the publisher at www.fourriverspress.com.

ISBN 978-0-9817698-3-7

Library of Congress Control Number: 2010922118

Library of Congress subject headings:
1 Consciousness. 2. Participant observation. 3. Phenomenology.
4. Philosophy of Mind. 5. Observation (Psychology) 6. Perception.
7. Transcendence (Philosophy).

To all those who,
alive amidst the walking dead,
dare to be awake.

List of Essays

Consciousness, or the Ubiquity of Trance 1

The Trance-Outs of Everyday Life, or Who's At Home in Your Body (When You're Not?) 17

The Ground of Knowing: The 'Psyche' as the Seat of Consciousness and Assembler of 'Reality' 37

The Extensions of Consciousness 49

The Consciousness of Intimacy 57

The Visual Play of Consciousness 65

The Consciousness of Familiarity/Unfamiliarity 93

Goose Bumps, Shivers & Body Slams: Embodying Consciousness's Exaltations 101

The Consciousness of Newness 109

The Consciousness of Grace 117

The Discontinuities of Consciousness 123

Dream Consciousness 129

Obsession and Possession Consciousness 137

The Consciousness of Meditation 151

Afterword: Intelligence Consciousness 161

Acknowledgements

From the earliest recognition that I possessed the possibility of thought, existential questions started nipping at the heels. *Who* am I? *Why* am I? Why is there *anything*? Sixty years later, the same questions continue to possess—and maybe plague—me. Yet, regardless of being sourced and ciphered in some unknown (and unknowable?) provenance, and currently held in a space-time current coursing me towards some unknown destiny (or, at the very least, a knowable fate), I have to acknowledge the richness that such grapplings with large questions have lent to my life.

The Psalmist's declarations in Psalm 139, verses 15 and 16, may come closest to fathoming the unfathomable:

> *15 My frame was not hidden from You,*
> *When I was made in secret,*
> *And skillfully wrought in the lowest parts of the earth.*

> *16 Your eyes saw my substance, being yet unformed.*
> *And in Your book they all were written,*
> *The days fashioned for me,*
> *When as yet there were none of them.*

In keeping with the Psalmist's sentiments, it is only fair to acknowledge the following: To *Whatever* has sourced me, and woven into my being the impetus, capacity, and (perhaps) audacity to take up and engage with such questions, I, as one would-be aware and conscious member of humankind, express my gratitude.

To be possessed of such questions means to be constantly on the lookout for any clues that may be garnered which may lend a hand in dispersing, a bit, the shroud of the unknown. Hence these variegated and curious essays, drawing on numerous encounters with unexceptional, readily accessible experiences of everyday life, within which, just perchance, there lay hints that, to the discerning consciousness, may be revealing of more pervasive, possibly transcendent underpinnings.

The essays comprising *Who's At Home...* aggregated, bit by bit, over the course of eighteen months or so. Along the way, swatches of them were shared with Hannah B. Merriman, H. D. Merriman, and Joely W. Merriman, resonant ears all. Larger swaths of whole cloth were shared with Brother Blue, of Cambridge, Massachusetts—a wonderful, loving presence (now recently departed) who devoted himself to the creation of compassionate human connection through use of parable and story, and Bill Ryan and Jeanne Lightfoot of Ashfield (Pioneer Valley), Massachusetts, who read the manuscript in its entirety and proffered helpful comments based on their own life encounters. Special thanks also go out to Doc and Patty Kuster of Bastrop, Texas, Donald Flach of San Francisco, California and Steve Simmer of Northampton, Massachusetts for their devoted and steadfast readings of several of my books over a number of years. It is an honor to have devoted and thoughtful readers who dare to be both alive and awake. Their encouragement has been heartwarming. I wish to express a special note of gratitude to Emily Sara Taylor Merriman, my wife, true love and partner in life, who (quite possibly) knows me (at times) better than I know myself. Emily, in addition to being my "in house" editor (on those all too infrequent occasions when I am brave enough, and smart enough, to be open to her skillful advice), also fashioned the haunting cover image for *Who's At Home...* My words fall woefully short of adequately recording the extent of my gratitude, love and sense of deep connection that her efforts bring forth in me.

Acknowledgement is also heartily expressed to Johnn O'Sullivan, in this context my copy editor, for his exacting eye, as well as helpful comments as to content and style. Johnn and I have collaborated on many projects over the years, ranging in scope from an alchemical admixture of poetry and music (Johnn O'Sullivan's CD: *SEEDS*), to his work on several of my books. Our friendship of over thirty-five years is a ripening vintage—an ongoing delight to me.

Finally, grateful acknowledgement is made to Tim Kinnel, of *words are images*, for his exemplary work in typesetting and book design for *Who's At Home...*, as well as his expert efforts on other offerings from Four Rivers Press.

While I assume sole (soul?) responsibility for the content of *Who's At Home...*, the book would never have made its way beyond being a mouldering, shelf-bound manuscript without this flow of collective love, support and encouragement. My gratitude is enduring to each of the aforementioned. Thank you all for helping to launch *Who's At Home...* into whatever destiny the outer world may hold for it.

Preface

Who's At Home In Your Body (When You're Not)? Essays on Consciousness by a Participant-Observer is comprised of a series of essays invoking some quirky, off-beat, yet nevertheless easily and widely observable and accessible domains of consciousness. While not, per se, an exhaustive work on consciousness (could ever such be written?), *Who's At Home...* does call attention to transcendent awarenesses and experiences encoded in a myriad of commonplace occurrences and phenomena generally overlooked by most participants—that is, by most of us. In drawing discriminating attention to such prosaic matters, *Who's At Home...* also unfurls some philosophical speculations as possible ramifications spurred on by these observations of the commonplace. These speculations, while not purporting to be "right," are designed to encourage you, my readers, to become observers of (in addition to already being de-facto participants in) consciousness—*your* consciousness.

As an observer of your own consciousness, you are invited to expand upon, refute, or otherwise embellish or diminish the scope of what is reported and reflected upon here, and to muse philosophical in whatever direction your own sense of implication carries you.

The observations that are set forth in the little essays that follow are *naturalistic* ones. No special requirement, aside from being alive and incarnate and in human form — come to think of it, these are highly specialized requirements! — well, no special qualifications (with the revised exception of the aforementioned) are required. No fancy, external apparati need be resorted to or employed. Naturalistic observation starts with the innate apparatus at hand: the unadorned body-sensorium, native intelligence (of whatever degree), and the motivation (however it is come by) to experience, observe, inquire of, and generate theory and meaning about whatever is before one.

Indeed, I'd like to think that these kinds of observations and speculations are native to any curious mind, regardless of cultural background, economic advantage or disadvantage, as well as the presence or lack of any formal education. Furthermore, I'd like to think that this kind of observing and philosophy-making is an inherent part of consciousness itself — maybe consciousness with an attitude: consciousness stuck on itself — and that this activity neither necessarily encourages nor discourages our drawing upon any additional education, background or training that may, however formally or haphazardly come by, also be in the picture. I'd even like to think that the application of self to observing and theory-making and philosophizing constitutes an innate training of mind (as promulgated by mind).

I'm convinced that, when it comes to observing, and making meaning of, one's own life, there are no amateur philosophers. *Everyone* is his own expert when called to the task of plumbing the depths of personal experience, and placing it in a context. At the level of generating personal meaning for our lives, we are all professionals.

So in a sense, this is an "every person's" (every woman's, every man's) book on consciousness. It's a "little person's" book. Its philosophical premise is that experiences of transcendence arise as a natural extension of our wakeful engagement with everyday reality, rather than as a prize for somehow successfully disregarding, escaping, evading or avoiding it. May this little book tease you and delight you and upset you, challenge you and support you. May it use the commonplace to lift you and your imagination out of the commonplace. May it transport you. May it lend dignity to your own strivings to fathom mystery and create meaning out of that—consciousness—in which, both individually and collectively, we are, each and every one of us, in every moment, immersed.

As in anything that issues from my pen, should you find yourself in the throes of *some* response to these writings, however strong (or weak) the impulse and regardless of the direction in which it veers (+ or -), my efforts shall have done their work.

Yours,
with love on our shared journey, and with my earnest respect for the inherent dignity of both our individual and shared consciousness,

Stephen Rich Merriman
Newton, Massachusetts
April 25th, 2002

Consciousness, or the Ubiquity of Trance[1]

One year when I was away at college (mid-1960s) I was really up against it. I'd been hitchhiking back and forth from the campus in Northern New England to Boston every autumn weekend trying, unsuccessfully, to resuscitate a romance, and had fallen behind in my work. Christmas break was approaching but I had exams to get through before I could take off—hit the interstate one more time with thumb outstretched—and head home—home, a place that, in those years, still held, for me, the delusional promise of reunion, restoration and hearth.

Impulsively, I decided to write a postcard to myself *as the person I knew I would be* when I would already have returned home and be receiving the very card I was to write. I instinctively knew that I was a very different person in Boston than I was as a grimly determined student caught in the isolation of a frozen, rural, fraternity-ridden, alcohol-soaked campus.

---

1) This chapter, and the one to follow, are adapted from chapters 1 and 2 in *Pathfinding Through Multiple Personality: Personal Reflections and Cumulative Perspectives on Trance, Dissociation, Treatment of Multiple Personality and Related Topics*, Doctoral Dissertation of Stephen Rich Merriman (Columbia Pacific University, San Rafael, CA, 1996.)

Who's At Home In Your Body (When You're Not)?

And so I wrote, imagining myself as the person to whom I was writing, and anticipating *his* joy at being the recipient of this card even as I wrote it. I congratulated the "Boston Stephen" for having made it through finals on the heels of a heart-broken fall.

I sent the card. A part of me, I knew, was already, through the night, traveling 220 miles southwards in the "H.P.O." (highway post-office vehicle)—already, in my mind's eye, making the transition to home and, I hoped, warmer climes. And then, steeling myself to endure, I took a break from my studies and set out alone into the cold night. I walked along some railroad tracks for several miles and then, restored through an elemental connection, returned to my work.

Some number of days later I was told that I had received a card in the mail, and it was then handed to me. I smiled. I mentally reached back to embrace that poor, yet determined, melancholic soul who had written me. We, I knew, shared an earnest, soulful joke of sorts, and a chuckle, and there was love and correspondence and mirth between us.

✧ ✧ ✧

Where is trance?... Everywhere. As considered from a certain perspective, there doesn't appear to be any state of consciousness that does not constitute a form of trance. At any given time some particular state of consciousness may be designated as a non-trance state, based on some consensual agreement

Consciousness, or the Ubiquity of Trance

as to what constitutes being "conscious" (as in for instance: "Real" consciousness is alert, while trance is sleep-like.). However, the so-called "non-trance," "real" consciousness state is often the very state of consciousness from within which the judgment about what constitutes non-trance is being formed! Indeed, the designation of what is genuine consciousness and what's merely trance is, I'm increasingly convinced, one of convenience only—and may, indeed, be nothing other than arbitrary—though admittedly not without utility.

Why this lead-off plunge into the notion that trance is everywhere? Well, there's really no insistence here that you take this to be so. However, I do encourage you to reflect upon the notion.

So here are some notions: Every time any of us goes through an entrance of any description—into a room, a courtyard, a museum, our place of work, a church, temple or mosque, a nightclub, a nature setting—into *any* environment—we are quite literally "en-tranced"—brought through an induction in which we are affected, even entrained, by the environment into which we are entering. Our state of consciousness undergoes an alteration or adjustment as it responds to the change—a change in consciousness, or, to put it differently, a change in the quality of trance in which we've been functioning.

This phenomenon takes on additional relevance when we enter—make an en-trance—into the interpersonal arena, for our own consciousness is affected not only by our entering a different environment physically, but also by the entrance into our own customary environment of *any* change or alteration, including, of course, the entrance of another person, as well as our entrance into any environment inclusive of a group of people.

Induction is a generic concept used, first and foremost, to describe the introduction of an electric current (alternating, or household current, in this example) and voltage into a coil of wire brought into proximity with another coil of wire in which voltage already exists and current is flowing. The coils in proximity are called, collectively, a transformer. As the current-carrying coil is brought into proximity with the non-current-carrying coil, the electromagnetic field of the first coil (the "primary") induces ("induction") a current in the coil of the second coil (the "secondary") and voltage can be measured there, despite the fact that there is no hard-wired connection between them.

Our little basic electricity induction analogy does not end here, however. As the second, originally non-energized coil of wire begins to be energized by the force field of the original coil, the current flow of the primary coil is also affected. It "comes under load," meaning that its own current flow becomes shaped by the presence of the second coil. One way of envisioning this is that once the second coil has commenced having its own current flow via proximity to the primary coil's electromagnetic field, the secondary coil's own current flow instantaneously generates its *own* electromagnetic

Consciousness, or the Ubiquity of Trance

field which extends out from the secondary coil and, in turn, affects the current flow in the primary coil, hence, "bringing it under load," or "loading it down"—influencing it.

This is the induction of basic electricity. What does it have to suggest to us, by way of analogy, about the pervasiveness of trance and induction as ineluctable qualities of life and consciousness? Most importantly, the fact that *induction, and therefore the alteration of any state of consciousness (trance state) is always a mutual or bi-directional process*. The current appearing in the secondary is a profound change via the presence of the current in the primary, and the resultant load-effect back upon the primary is, in its own way, as profound a change in the current pattern of the primary as is the inducement of current in the secondary.

Could it be that in the arena of interpersonal relations, specifically regarding any two interacting individuals, the force-field of trance in one person is always accompanied by an induced trance (altered) state in another person, who then proceeds, in turn, to induce trance in the first person, and on and on? We might term the overall effect, which is so instantly bi-directional and multilayered, as "co-trance." Considerable attention, within traditional hypnosis, is usually given to the unidirectional influence of one person's imposition upon another person's consciousness, but not much attention is rendered the complete interaction, in which both individuals' states of consciousness are altered.

The overall current loop constitutes a bi-directional linkage replete with feedback:

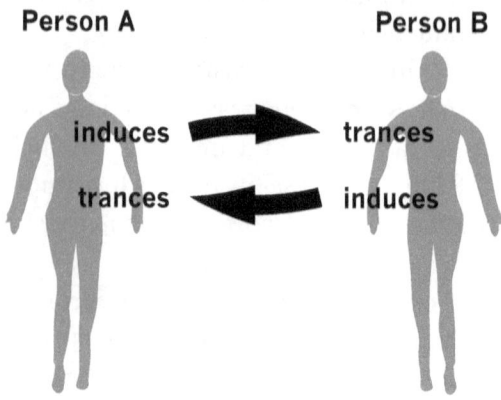

Inductions can happen to us without our being aware of them. *In fact, most inductions are of this sort.* They involve subtle changes—and sometimes not so subtle changes—in consciousness or trance that incessantly encroach upon the assumed observational resiliency of ego-consciousness. Our ego-consciousness—our "I-ness"—can't track them, nor do we, in ego form, necessarily even attempt to do so, being, instead, generally much taken with (and taken in by) our own unquestioned assumptions about the cinder-block solidity of our observations, and the firmness and stability of our own vantage point in making our observations.

Notwithstanding any such assumptions, in engaging in any interpersonal contact, no matter how polite, discrete or at-a-remove such an exchange may appear, all interactions occur within a context of layers of pre-existing and simultaneously arising co-trance and mutual induction as givens to relating—and these, which rise up spontaneously and unbidden at every turn, are not generally under any conscious scrutiny by either of the individuals involved. As already mentioned, the respective ego-consciousnesses of the interacting individuals are simply not in a self-observation trance monitoring state-shifts at all. Rather, their respective ego consciousnesses are operating, all the while, within their own discrete, separate trances, implicitly labeled (under the heading of) "stable objectivity."

The malleability of the consciousness between two relating individuals—the comings and goings of spells and trances on every side via co-trance—even as each person proceeds along under an encapsulating spell of supposed local objectivity, is one of the most important features in all of human interdynamics.

To truly recognize the impermanence, the transiency and the inconsistency of any apparently stable thought-frame of objectivity within oneself and about oneself is the beginning of true wisdom in what we might designate as the field of "consciousness relativity."

Another aspect of the pervasiveness of trance that bears mentioning is that *any state of consciousness*—discrete gestalt of consciousness—*while operative, carries within itself its own assumption that it constitutes the resident, presiding state of non-trance*—i.e., the genuine article of stable awareness—*and that every other state of consciousness, other than itself, is to be regarded as a "trance" or "altered" state.* I hinted at this characteristic of consciousness in the brief vignette that opened this essay. Indeed, this assumption seems to be an inherent feature of consciousness itself, and constitutes a further reason why the tracking of shifts of consciousness or trance states within oneself is so difficult. Such "changes of mood" can be tolerated under the operative assumption that the stable "I" presides, somehow, over the whole melange of mood and mentation. "Changes in mood" become harder to fathom if customary ego-consciousness has to begin to take *into itself* the consideration that such a trance shift involves not only a quality subordinate to itself, but also, *the supraordinate principle of organization governing its very awareness—ego consciousness—*and therefore its own capacity to track consciousness! "If I'm trying to get to know myself (track my own states of consciousness), then I'm trying to get to know the person who's trying to get to know me (trying to get to know the person who's trying to track my own states of consciousness)" is a statement—a kind of mind-tease—that points to this dilemma.

This habitual assumption by our resident state of awareness consciousness—our "I"-ness—by *each* of us—that we (each of us individually in ego-form) constitute a non-trance state or condition, leads readily to some very unhelpful interactions in the realm of our relating with other people.

Consciousness, or the Ubiquity of Trance

First, and most troublesome, is the almost automatic, unreflecting assumption—an unquestioned assertion, really—that any other person with whom we interact is a singularity, when, at the outset, the only singular fact about a person we can bank on is the existence of one body. We reflexively impose and stencil our concept of unitary consciousness, as we assume it exists within us, onto other people because of the personal convenience it affords us in so doing. This is born of the unexamined assumption either that pluralistic consciousness does not exist or that, even if it does, then at some level all constituent elements, or consciousnesses, within a person must "really know what's going on" as part of an overarching singularity. This is a polite, fraudulent fiction.

We also make similar, unhelpful errors in implicitly deciding, right out of a vacuum, to anoint whatever side of a person we first meet and get to know as the organizing principle of that person, simply because *that* manifestation of the person's personhood is the one we just happen to encounter (and, often, get taken in by!) at the outset.

Our insistence in dealing with a person as if that person, in essence, functions as a unitary singularity can have pernicious consequences. Other sides of a person and their relevance to an emergent, evolving, more comprehensive experience of that person are not given their due. This exclusion inevitably leads to a woefully deficient and impoverished experience of another, in which her/his richness and variability are simply not taken into account. A person becomes pigeonholed—and locked by our own expectations—into a one-dimensional mold, and we miss the whole show of discovering the multidimensional richness within that person (*Every* person has, and is, this.).

Another aspect of the pervasiveness of trance that is well worth noting involves state-dependent learning and recollection. With the procession of trance states—our shifting consciousness—in which we are each daily immersed, come experiences that are specific to each discrete state of trance.

As a typical (so far as I can tell) human services practitioner with an unexceptional range of activities, I am daily deluged by innumerable details and nuances spread across the range of interpersonal interactions that cross my path during any batch of hours. Although I usually keep notes of various encounters, the actual capacity to record and preserve the minutiae—even the important minutiae—of various meetings and exchanges is lacking, and even if such a recording task were to be done, I would never have the time to retrieve and review the data and detail stored about each person I encounter.

What I noticed some years ago (long before I had recognized the realities of co-trance and pluralistic consciousness) is that when in the presence of each person (read: with my sequencing into the induction—the wakeful trance ambient for each person), the detail, the nuance, the minutiae, the

Consciousness, or the Ubiquity of Trance

"experiential recollection"—*all* would be there for me to draw on. Personal information involving those with whom I would interact was stored within me in a trance-specific way, encoded within the overall state of consciousness I would carry respective to each person. Nor would I be able, necessarily, to recall other than the broad outlines of detail or circumstance once a consultation was concluded, and co-trance was no longer operative regarding a specific person. All of this alteration of consciousness/trance was virtually automatic, and certainly operative during years of professional work long before I ever became aware of it.

I also discovered during this period that while learning that was acquired within a given state of trance could be carried over to a subsequent state of consciousness, the translation *always* involved effort, and something of the "experiential completeness" of the interactions encountered while in the prior state of consciousness—within the trance state resident to the experience (the trance state in which the encounter with the person took place)—was *always* lost in translation.

Easier, in a way, to have an experience in a trance-specific state, establish a minimalistic "table of contents" file (so to speak) in a subsequent state of consciousness which would reference the earlier trance-specific experience, and then be able to *return* to the trance state specific to the experience once again (as needed) to work with the details and material of the experience.

One straightforward example of the efficiency of (1) learning, or acquiring, information within one specific state of consciousness, (2) simultaneously storing, or filing that information within the *same* state of consciousness, (3) referencing the existence of that state-specific experience in a subsequent state of consciousness, and (4) then returning, at will, to the prior state of consciousness to access, participate in, and use the information (rather than translate the knowledge into a different state of consciousness for storage and retrieval and utilization) is the common situation of the two-car family. Each car drives very differently. The clutches (we drive manual transmission cars), brakes, arrangement of the gearboxes, gear ratios, torque ranges of the engines, road feel, and so on, are markedly different for each car. Yet the kinesthetic gestalt of driving for each car, *once learned* for each one, remains stored within the encoded experience of actually driving each car, and does not have to be relearned.

This is to say that a person climbing into the car s/he drives less often, but "knows" how to drive (having been through the learning curve with that car at some prior time), goes, seamlessly, through an induction and into trance (the state-specific trance of driving that particular car) and, once induced, has instant access to the learned/absorbed gestalt (the kinesthetics) the *feel* of the experience of driving that particular car,

Consciousness, or the Ubiquity of Trance

without much hesitation. It's "all" there.

While one could think about it ahead of time—i.e., make a translation of the prior kinesthetic experience of driving the car into cognitions within one's non-driving state of consciousness) about "how the clutch grabs lower in my spouse's car and the brakes pump harder and the shift box is arranged differently"—this would be a very inefficient use of conscious resources. Far easier, and efficient, to revisit the trance—the resident (albeit utilitarianly transient) state of consciousness—in which the information (the total experience of driving that specific car) is both stored and available, and then just utilize it.

The notion of state-dependent/trance-specific learning and recollection as an important subset of the ubiquity of trance is an invaluable awareness to carry into all our interactions with other people. While it is probably true that there is a range of pluralistic consciousness in which the procession of trances and attendant states of consciousness proceeds under the confines of a more or less stable frame of ego-consciousness—of "I"-ness—it is humbling to have to acknowledge that the illusoriness of the actual constancy of our ability to attend, and the shakiness of the faith we may take for granted as to the validity of the cognitions and constancy of our attending consciousness, apply just as much to us as it does to those with whom we would interact. Our implicit, habitual, reflexive assumptions about humankind—that we are all, at heart, unitary and cohesive, need to give way to a more encompassing assessment of just how pluralistic and "trancy" human life and consciousness really are—every day and in every wakeful moment!

Some caveats for reflection that I have found helpful:

(1) Don't assume that any state of consciousness—no matter how permanent, enduring, immutable, grounded or "real" it may *seem*—is not a trance state (including the state of consciousness you are in at this very moment as you read these words).

(2) Don't assume that any state of consciousness, no matter how ephemeral or transient, won't *feel* just as immanent and permanent as any grounded ego-state (and have a feeling of constancy akin to such a state) *while it is in effect.*

(3) Recognize that the convention of designating some states of consciousness as "trance" states and other states of consciousness as "non-trance" states is arbitrary, though provisionally useful at times.

(4) Try to recognize that co-trance, as an interpersonal dynamic and phenomenon, is ever operative within your relations with others with or without your consent. (Shifts in your consciousness accompany shifts in consciousness in others, and shifts initiating within their consciousness will induce you into trance just as readily as your shifts affect them. This is stated just for the purpose of reemphasizing the bi-directionality of induction.)

(5) Try to be mindful that whatever state of consciousness or trance is present within you will tend

Consciousness, or the Ubiquity of Trance

to don the mantle of non-trance, presenting itself as "the genuine article"—and that trance states or altered states will therefore be designated as being whatever states of consciousness are *not* currently present.

(6) Become aware of the inductions—the "entrances"—of your everyday world, your absorption into countless different environments throughout the course of a day. (Try to track the inductions a bit—from a mood-state change induced by hearing a certain piece of music, perhaps, to a kinesthetic change in the body during rush-hour driving, to patterns of response and feeling around certain individuals whom you encounter, to awareness of shifting patterns and moods as you move through the micro-environments of your daily life.)

(7) Try to pose the following questions to yourself at least several times during the day: "Is the 'I' making such assessments of my daily progression of trance states independent of the equation (an independent variable)? Is it (am I!) such a constant, unaltered observational faculty as I track my trances—my procession of consciousnesses? ... Or am 'I' impacted by the very question I pose—even by the very act of posing it, or by the act of observation itself—and affected or changed in some particular?" And then ask yourself these questions: "Is the 'I' now posing these questions about my trance states the same 'I' who asked these questions earlier in the day? Do I feel like the same 'I'?"

(8) Reflect on whether there is knowledge within

you that is state-specific/trance-specific—i.e., bases of information or ranges of thought, feeling or physical capabilities which become available to you as you move into their domain and enter into those states of trance which are resident to them.

> *What is man that thou art mindful of him?*
> —Psalm 8: The Book of Psalms

> *What is it that, of which to be mindful, you yourself must be?*
> —Another way of asking the same question

The Trance-Outs of Everyday Life, or Who's At Home in Your Body (When You're Not?)[1]

When I was a young child, I would, occasionally, play in the street during rainstorms. We lived on a gentle hillside, and the water run-off would quickly fill up the curbs; very occasionally, the sewer on the corner of Avon Hill and Hillside would overflow. I especially liked to place the notched-ended sticks of Tinker Toy into the curbside currents and watch them go.

The Tinker Toy sticks would follow the current around obstacles—rocks, other large sticks or clumps of leaves, and during melting season, the dissolving mounds of snow and ice (sometimes disappearing down sluices sculpted under ledges of eroding, undercut ice, and magically reappearing downstream). It always seemed to me that the little dowelled sticks just "knew" where the obstacles were and could, at the last moment—of their own volition—veer this way or that around obstructions and continue to course down the freshet. Once in a great while the sewer would overflow, sending a whole other level of torrent down the curbs. This was the most exciting time of all!

---

1) Please see footnote 1 on p. 1.

One rainy day, when I was about six years old, I was once again along the street with my sticks of Tinker Toy. I stood across from the sewer, hoping and wishing that it would overflow (although the rain hadn't been all that heavy, and there was no sign that it would). Suddenly, within the consciousness of this young child, magic struck!

With no prior indication that the sewer was near to overflowing, I nevertheless found myself instantaneously placed in that same scene, only a moment before wishing upon a simple rainstorm, and now, an instantaneous moment later, standing in the midst of an inundation already well underway—the whole street gushing with water, a large pool with concentric wavelets spreading out from the sewer, and small, yet definite tidal combers caroming off the curbs and berserking down the gullies. I was in water-heaven! My wish had come true—all in an instant!

This sudden switch in water-realities only happened once. Over the following years of childhood on up into my forties, I reflected upon this experience from time to time. Memory did not diminish the "magic"—or the mystery—in it. Eventually the sense of mystery surrounding this occasion yielded to the mystery of an explanation—in its own way no less mysterious.

✧ ✧ ✧

Dissociation is the ability to "vanish" to, or vacate from, current experience, even while that experience is occurring. In other words (to put the matter most generically), a person is dissociated from everything to which she or he is not consciously attending. By definition, this implies that *we are all in a continual, dissociated state, relative to that which is not held as a conscious focus*. Of course, as pointed out in the previous chapter, the thread of our "I"-ness (our ego-consciousness) creates such an illusion of continuity in our awareness that we, within any moment, are not aware that there could be anything else happening to which we might attend—AND, therefore, given this lack of basic recognition, we can not even be aware that we are not attending to it. Each experiential moment of awareness, regardless of how narrow or broad its actual range of focus, usually carries along with it its own sense of sufficiency and completeness as a conscious experience.

And yet, questioned or unquestioned, the dissociations of everyday life surround us, and sometimes their manifestations are quite bold, if we would but consider. For instance, the last time you were driving in your car from point 'A' to point 'B' and were rapt in thought on some other matter of the day, only to become aware within some instant that you were nearly arrived at your destination, you were (had been) dissociating—you were vanishing to a current experience the body was engaged in even as that experience was happening. Can you consciously recollect traversing the intersections and negotiating the other traffic which would have been encountered along the way? Probably not. "You" weren't there.

Who was "at home" in the body while you were consciously vacated—while your conscious attention—indeed, your ego experience—indeed, *you*, were "relocated"—were elsewhere? Were you any more present, or more functional, for instance, than a "blackout" drinker who, while under the influence of alcohol may appear, to observers, as functional, ambulatory, aware and consciously engaged in reality only to have, subsequently, no conscious recollection of what transpired during the "blackout" interval?

Indeed, while *I* was driving from point 'A' to point 'B', I *was* having an experience: I was "with my thoughts," as arising spontaneously or as influenced by other stimuli (such as the induction of music playing in my car, or becoming engrossed in a talk radio show). It is not that I broke off having a conscious life—only that my conscious life broke off from being engaged with a particular range of external reality, in this case the driving of my car.

Again, who, on such an occasion, is driving? The facile answer is, "I am." However, this answer is misleading because, as already mentioned, the thread of ego-consciousness—"I"—is elsewhere, and not attending to the task. So who's in the driver's seat while "I" am not? Who's "at home" (in the body) while I'm not?

Let's consider this question in a bit more detail. Driving a car involves the kinesthetic knowledge of driving combined with a remarkable array of sophisticated judgment calls involving the activities (and predictions of those activities) of other drivers, as well as a host of other variables. While the themes (so to speak) of driving may be finite, the possible variations on these themes are virtually infinite, and ever changing and rearranging. Whoever or whatever is present to attend to this level of complexity during my absence—my "absent-mindedness" (my mind is absent the body!) or my "relocating" ('I' am elsewhere!)—has a profound set of capabilities which are apparently quite autonomous—able to function suitably without being consciously directed by the body's usual resident "I." (Indeed, at such times my body is truly "pre-occupied"—quite readily, in my absence, occupied by another consciousness!)

If one takes this conundrum of the "vacant 'I'" seriously, it may be worthwhile (and necessary) to consider whether or not consciousness is intrinsically pluralistic. This same question could be posed about our very being: the 'I' that may be a kind of 'We.'

Please note that I'm not hinting at anything that would be regarded as clinically significant dissociation or multiple personality disorder (now officially dubbed "dissociative identity disorder"). Thus far, the implications in my dissociation example and the mere hint of there existing "multiplicity" dimensions to our state of being are adaptive, not maladaptive. They may be considered as "how things are"—as simply the routine the state of affairs—rather than as pathological deviations from the normal.

Who's At Home In Your Body (When You're Not)?

Perhaps the "who" who's there when I'm not—who "pre-occupies" me—is not a singular presence. Perhaps this "who" is capable of engaging with the outer world over a range competencies, covering a spectrum of presence(s), from a kinesthetic, perceptually and cognitively aware "problem solver" (more like the artificial, programmed "intelligence" of robotics) on the one hand, to some presence who is capable of semi-competent interpersonal interactions (as in when, for instance, "I" am tranced out with boredom and not attending closely to being around, and interacting with, someone I don't care for), even as the conversational exchange is somehow being maintained.

Our dream life and what we know of the mind through the study of free association and parapraxes (slips of the tongue, the pen, and so on—the "Freudian slips" of everyday life) suggest the existence of co-operative (though not always cooperative) trains of logical thought which are discrete and independent of our conscious thought train. But the "presence" (which I have noted above) takes on the additional characteristic of being able to exert *a functional intention, within the body itself,* during our everyday wakeful lives, in the absence of the resident "I." This, of course, does not mean that such presence(s) may not also be operative within the body while the resident "I" is "at home." Under the latter circumstance, however, such presences would presumably be harder to detect as singularities in the midst of an amalgam with, or co-presence with, the resident "I."

Thus far I have spoken of dissociation as a normal occurrence, as indeed it is—a capacity each one of us has and is involved with continuously. The dissociative capacity works in and through and around us, usually quite seamlessly. We are fully acclimated to it without, for the most part, taking any note of it.

Let's thicken the plot a bit. If we see dissociation as simply another form of trance into which one may be induced, or gain en-trance to, what are some of the indications that can lead to significant manifestations of it? In milder form (as in daydreaming and fantasizing), dissociation can be brought on by: fatigue, boredom, enthrallment; aesthetic stimulation, ascetic stimulation, mortification or non-stimulation (sensory deprivation); anxiety, sense of foreboding; sense of eager anticipation, enthusiasm; sexual arousal, recreational drug/alcohol use; physical exercise, accidents, and so on. In more pronounced forms (to be described more fully shortly), dissociation may be brought on by experiences of profound sensory/cognitive overload and inundation, and experiences of profound sensory/cognitive deprivation and neglect.

Experiences of profound sensory/cognitive overload can include: combat fatigue (the original, recognized form of post-traumatic stress) and its inner-city or terrorism-related equivalents; accidents (especially those experienced as life-threatening); illnesses (ditto); exaltations (successes or victories, as in sports or career); "fight, flight or freeze" experiences (adrenaline); sudden experiences of unanticipated failure, public humiliation or shame, or sudden experiences of unanticipated public praise and affirmation; prolonged confinement; childhood incest/physical/sexual abuse/sadism; childhood experiences of sensory/cognitive overload, or childhood experiences of sensory/cognitive deprivation.

In profound dissociation-precipitating experiences a person is less likely to be progressively (incrementally) entrained by her/his own thought pattern into a trance of inattention to the body and its involvement with the physical world (typical of milder dissociation), and more likely to be hurtled into it ("splitting") as an artifact of consciously trying to counter, or avoid—get out of the way of—some suddenly encroaching, overwhelmingly compelling inundation or onslaught. When such a severe dissociative manifestation is underway, it may be experienced by the formerly residing/now rapidly exiting (the body) consciousness as a complete alteration of time and space and identity, or as a more or less sustained identity but with an out-of-body (and therefore "removed") vantage point, or as a retreating deep within the body to a place of refuge, sanctuary or hiding, or all of these simultaneously! Outer manifestations of a more pronounced dissociative experience (if an observer is there to witness) may be complete catatonia (an apparently utterly vacant body), or extreme manifestations of emotion (terror, shrieking, hysterical laughter, etc.) which subsequently prove to be non-ego connected (there's no recollection of them later), or some presence of conscious, mobilized defense in the body (possibly in the form of a personality or separate ego-state).

This leads us to consider consciousness as "memory" — specifically, how "memory" is partitioned or allocated during a pronounced dissociative episode, and, as we shall see, during *any* experience, not just traumatic ones.

Consider the experience you are having right now as you read what I've written. (I'm having my own analogous experience while I'm writing this.) Just what are the components that go into the make-up of a complete experience? Well, there are probably many. However, for our purposes let's consider three basic ones.

First, while you're reading this, your thinking/thought process is obviously engaged (I hope!). The words you are reading form sentences which present thoughts that shape and present concepts. To some extent your "thinking" is engaged as you read and consider this material, regardless of whether the writing appears to hold together or not. We might term this aspect of experience the "cognitive level" of experience.

It's amazing to recognize (once one starts to notice such things) how many people just assume, without ever questioning the premise, that the cognitive level constitutes virtually *all* of what an experience (and the memory of an experience) is, or consists of. To recall an experience is, for these people, to conjure up a sequence of events intellectually, to "remember" an occurrence—something that took place, and to remember as well *that* something took place. Such recollections are often cast in a context of chronology—a linear progression of some sort. Yet at best, the cognitive/rational/thinking faculty—as important as it is to "knowing" and recollection—accounts for, at most, about one-third (and probably a bit less) of the consciousness of a complete experience, as well as the memory of that experience.

Second, as you read this writing, what is your body doing? Are you lying down or are you sitting? Is the body comfortable in its posture, or is it tense? Is it in a slouch, or is it more upright? Does it shift around a lot (legs crossing back and forth, for instance) as in trying to keep you awake?… Or does it feel heavy and want to doze off? *Whatever* your body is doing or not doing, and *however* it feels kinesthetically (muscle tone: certain groups of muscles tensing, certain groups of muscles slacking) and *however* the body's sensory faculties are being used (including the visual, the olfactory, taste, auditory as well as tactile or touch)—all of this is your body's *own* experience—*its own consciousness*—of the same experience which you (resident "I") and your body are having simultaneously as you consciously read this. In other words, the body is having, and is providing you with, its own component (about one-third) of the total experience you are having as you plow through this.

Third, what about your capacity of *feeling*—the emotion, the "affective" component? Just what feelings are you having while you are reading this? Are you bored to tears by such a minute dissection of such an utterly uncompelling experience? (I won't take it personally.) Conversely, are you stimulated or energized by the intellectual content of the ideas? Are you feeling a bit pissed off or annoyed at the ponderousness of the writing style and by an apparent attitude (perhaps bordering at times on glibness) on the part of the writer?... Or do you feel somewhat enthused about the cadence of the writing and the cascading, sort of lurching quality of the (alleged) thought process? Are you offended by the premises that "Everywhere is trance" and that "Someone is home" in your body when "you" aren't?... Or are you amused to be encountering a kind of novel, quirky way of looking at things? *Whatever* your palette of feelings may be as you read these paragraphs—whatever emotional hues are evoked—*is* the feelings component of the experience you are having of taking in this material, and your affective experience chips in approximately one-third to the overall experience you are currently having, and to the memory of that experience.

What I hope is becoming clear to you as you are having the experience that you're having *right now* is that *each* faculty—the cognitive/rational, the somatic/sensory, and the affective/feeling/emotive—is having its *own discrete experience* of what, as viewed from the outside, looks like a unified single activity: your reading this stuff. The three components may pool resources and orchestrate a complete experience—the overall experience itself. However, regardless of whether or not there is such an orchestration, *each component of experience is also being stored discretely and separately from the others, and constitutes its own level of memory.*

In particular, the capacity of the body to store its own form of memory, including its kinesthetic and sensory gestalts, is something to which not much attention is paid, but that can turn out to be of considerable importance for many of us—for example, those who "mysteriously" develop physical symptoms of one sort or another, often in the absence of any "logical" explanation as to their origin.

Yet the presence of body-encoded experience and memory-consciousness should not really be all that surprising when one considers that in, for instance, the midst of any physical onslaught (accidents, bodily illness, physical or sexual abuse, and so on), when major dissociative phenomenology is kicking into gear (the consciousness of experience is splitting along the cognitive/somatic/affective axes), *the body can not vacate the body.* It remains present to whatever is being inflicted on it, and it continues to encode into its own form of memory the kinesthetic and evolving sensory state of the body which constitute its experience of the trauma.

Consequently, it should be greeted as no surprise, whether entertained theoretically or encountered empirically, that the upwelling of physical symptoms and sensory images—i.e., the body's consciousness of the complete experience—its own particular form of awareness—may be the first component of memory or recollection to surface in a person who has a history of some form of past trauma, *in the absence, initially, of any other surfacing components (the cognitive and affective) that, along with "body memory," are always constituent residues of having such a history*.

Though initially utterly ego-dystonic—for there is usually, at the outset (and onset) no "conscious," rational memory (no cognitive information supporting the existence) of such a history—and though routinely treated only symptomatically within the purview of traditional allopathic medicine—such body symptoms are, under auspicious circumstances, often the precursors to a fuller surfacing of the other components of memory-consciousness, as well. This spontaneous upwelling of physical symptoms and sensory images within an apparent vacuum of cognitive knowing is one of the least appreciated, and most misread, occurrences within contemporary Western medicine.

As earlier mentioned, the encoding by the body of its own range of experience, both kinesthetic and sensory, as "body memory" does not only happen during a rapid dissociation-engendering trauma. *Such encodings of memory-consciousness are continuous, and ongoing, moment by moment*.

Many years into my studies as an observer of consciousness (really, unavoidably, as participant-observer), I noted an experience within me which highlighted for me just how exquisitely *sensitive* the body's discrete memory-encoding process can be.

I had noted for a number of months that when I was just starting to get drowsy and fall off to sleep, I would experience a feeling of slight disorientation in space — almost random micro-movements throughout the body accompanied by equally minor, yet definite, sensations of being slightly disoriented and out of physical equilibrium, which I would — or the body would — instantly counteract and correct. I mean, the experience was extremely subtle. These experiences remained a mystery to me for some time and, beyond noting their occurrence, I viewed them as a benign enigma.

Many months later I was hiking in some hills and, at the wooded summit of one of those rises, I realized that if I could gain about another twenty feet of altitude, my sight-line would clear a ridge to the west, and I would be rewarded with an unobstructed view.

I found a climbable white pine, grappled my way up and around branches, gaining another thirty feet or so of height, and achieved my goal — a truly breathtaking panorama. Feeling moved by the experience, and securely straddling an upper crotch in the tree, I decided to meditate there, leaning my upper body along a length of the pine's upper trunk, with my arms loosely clasped around it to secure me. As I gently meditated into a slightly relaxed state, with eyes closed, *I became aware of the identical movements in the body which I had earlier noted in my pre-sleep state.* Only this time, it was the gentle movement of the wind through the tree, and the resulting multitude of micro-movements which each little area of the tree was undergoing, that my body was now feeling: tons of sinuous micro-disalignments and realignments as the trunk and branches all moved in ten thousand different directions at once.

All in a moment, I at once knew that this was the body's memory-consciousness, for it came to me instantly that as a child I had often taken refuge from a turbulent family environment by going outside and climbing a white pine adjacent to the house, where I had secured myself in the top-most branches and let myself be lulled and soothed by the breeze, the view and the rocking of the tree.

If the body can encode and, a number of decades later, serve up its version — its body-consciousness — of such a subtle experience with such exactitude, there should be little doubt as to its capacity to encode, and independently serve up, its own form of memory regarding a vast array of equally slight and subtle, as well as more pronounced, events and experiences.

In devoting considerable attention to bodily aspects of dissociation, I have probably underemphasized the significance of dissociation as it can invoke the cognitive and affective faculties. Indeed, cognitive memory-consciousness and affective memory-consciousness are, in their own turn, just as separate and autonomous in their rumblings and potential unruliness as anything body-consciousness can serve up.

For instance, in the surfacing of the affective/emotive component of a prior traumatic experience, we have, in its own way, the equivalent of what was earlier described regarding the surfacing of somatic memory-consciousness. In the latter example a body symptom of some sort would breach cognitive awareness and be experienced as alien, out of context and therefore disorienting because there would be no conscious referent—no cognitive historical reference—to an historical antecedent which could "explain" the symptom—that is, place it in a rational context. Similarly, in such an apparent *lack* of context a surfacing of affective/emotive-consciousness is *just* as disorienting as the previous example involving body-consciousness, only in lieu of a physical symptom we have an emotional current, mood, or sometimes, even, a flooding of feeling which appears to have no conscious reason to be there. This experience can be equally disconcerting and compelling.

Also of note is that while the cognitive/rational consciousness may have no awareness of past traumatic events, there are some forms of dissociation in which cognitive memory *is* operative to some extent. One often discovers, in such instances, that although a conscious memory trace of an event may remain—a person may recall that "such and such happened"—the cognitive component (the rational/conscious memory) is often completely devoid of any emotional or somatic content. In such instances rational consciousness is reporting at a profound remove from any emotional of bodily concomitants. Such an account is rendered as affectively flat, and the whole experience, as reported, is presented as somehow distant or removed, and of not much relevance—just "something that happened," or "happened to happen," and of no particular import. It's almost as if one is hearing a "disembodied" account; there is no vitality to the presentation or reported recollection; the reported sense is almost as if "it happened to someone else, not to me."

If we observe such a style of recollection in others, and subsequently see how such cognitive memory-consciousness falls far short of reporting on (what may later prove to have been) a markedly fuller, compelling range of experience, it may give *us* pause the next time we catch ourselves "remembering" some aspect of our *own* past experience in a way that seems in some way minimizing, trivializing, emotionally neutral, removed, matter of fact, or somatically detached.

In drawing to a close this essay on dissociation and other states of consciousness resident to the body simultaneous to the absence (and even presence) of "I"-ness—ego-consciousness—it's important to highlight once again that we all dissociate, or trance out. In other words, we all partition our orchestrated consciousness into a number of discrete forms. This capacity is innate, and non-pathological. In its origins it is adaptive, and at its best it remains so. Even multiple personality (of the clinical sort[2], usually taken as an extreme manifestation of dissociation, is not necessarily pathological, provided it remains (or through treatment becomes) helpfully adaptive.

The dissociative capacity, overall, becomes a "disorder" only at the point beyond which it exhibits maladaptive qualities, and negative consequences ensue. If you start to trance while driving and wind up with traffic fines, speeding tickets and accidents, then you will know that *that* level of dissociation has become maladaptive (and clinically significant). If, for instance, a conflict-ridden person makes, from the direction of the purely cognitive/rational level of consciousness, single-handed and willful claims as to what *should* be happening in the life of the body, as well as his/her emotional life, and categorically repudiates any other "claims" as might be forthcoming (in the form of "symptoms") from these other resident consciousnesses, then internal civil war is the result, and the "disorder" part of trancing out appears.

While it may be unsettling to grapple with the notion that our body carries within it at least several different consciousnesses that are co-present and simultaneously operative along with us in our more accustomed "I"-ness form—*and* autonomously present and operative in the body during those occasions when we in "I"-ness form are vacant—the evidence that this is so in your own life is right there, awaiting your

---

[2] Now (re)named, "officially" (DSM-IV) as dissociative identity disorder.

observation and discovery.

As increasingly conscious beings one of our largest callings is to be open to the vast richness of the different consciousnesses which reside, and coexist, within us, recognizing that they are all a part of our inner panoply of selfhood. This selfhood—*our* selfhood—is, and always has been, *pluralistic*. Increasing consciousness of, along with the humility that ensues from, the realization that "one does not live *for* oneself alone"—and, perhaps, more especially, that "one does not live *by* oneself alone"—can assist us in "deepening relations" with these other intelligences and their own forms of knowing, behaving, experiencing and remembering that abide with, and within, us. Establishing and deepening relations, over time, can help in the conscious inclusion and collaborative shaping of these capacities into increasingly adaptive and internally cooperative assets, even as we (in "I"-ness form) become, ourselves, increasingly incorporated into their world—and no less reshaped by these encounters as we come to experience different aspects of *their* vitality.

Within such mutual assimilation—fraught with mystery, wonder and the not-yet-known—lies a path to personal mastery, wholeness and meaning.

Who's At Home In Your Body (When You're Not)?

The Ground of Knowing: The 'Psyche' as the Seat of Consciousness and Assembler of 'Reality'

The place whence you peer into space
Is a space beyond all time and place,
From which you gaze minus a trace
Of knowing your essential face.

What if the "you" who looks through your eyes actually has its abode in—and "looks" out from—a timeless, spaceless "place" called "psyche?"

"Psyche," the root stem of the word "psychology," means "soul." As a construct posited as undergirding and perfusing every aspect of our being, and shaping any reality in which we participate, it is seminal to postulate "psyche" as the organ of perception itself: the very seat of consciousness. If we designate the psyche as an organ, however, it is a strange one indeed, for no one has ever seen, outright, a "psyche."

And yet, as a consequence of postulating, however tentatively, the existence of the psyche as the seat of consciousness and assembler of reality, there arise all manner of intriguing notions, some of which may actually contribute to a greater understanding of consciousness and our relationship to it.

First, if the psyche is the organ of perception and

the seat of consciousness, then it is, possibly, the organ that assembles any and all information that reaches it—that makes an impression on it—into a mosaic which we take for granted as "our reality." This is not to minimize the extraordinarily complex functions that our own neurology plays in the generating and processing of percepts. It is to suggest, however, that our embodied neurology, with all that it does, constitutes a transducer of percept registration into forms that are rendered dimensionality and the contours of "personal reality" by "psyche" itself, and therefore is relatively subordinate to it. Psyche, however, while intimately related to "body" and neurology, ultimately both underlies and subsumes them—and is itself vastly "larger" than either, given the immensity of that which constantly impresses upon it and emanates from it. This view of things signifies nothing short of the notion that, notwithstanding neurology's special role, EVERYTHING we experience is therefore psychical—*of the psyche*—cognitioned through the psyche's very registration of it, assembling of it and presentation of it into that which is knowable—knowable as that which is known.

With the postulation of the psyche as the organ of input registration and reality-assembling, the distinction between what constitutes our so-called wakeful reality and our sleep-time reality—dreams—becomes a bit altered, for the very psyche that assembles and assimilates our wakeful states is the one that assembles and assimilates our dreams as well. *Every* event, whether

The Ground of Knowing

apparently of sleeping or wakeful origin, renders an impression on the psyche by which it is therefore known — by which 'we' consequently know it.

If the psyche in its role as the organ of perception and reality-assembler blurs the hard and fast distinction between "sleeping" and "wakeful" reality (given that it is the same organ assembling both realities), so does it also relativize the distinction between "concrete" — i.e., of the body and the external world — and "mental" — i.e., interior, of the mind and characterized by the realities of mental activity (comprised of thinking, abstract or otherwise, as well as some feeling states). The common denominator is that the psyche receives input — is impressed upon by data ("input") — from *whatever* source, and *that* datastream registers within the psyche, which is the only way (according to this way of looking at things) that any of us can know, or experience, *anything*.

A further notion that attaches to the psyche as the registrar of any and all inputs, and the fashioner of these inputs into our experiential frame, is that it is a transparent organ — that is, it does not readily give us evidence of its independent existence — it doesn't show us directly that *it* is operating. The psyche, in short, never gives its own coordinates away (nor, apparently, is it a part of its function to do so), but it provides us with *all* of ours. Therefore, we can't but take for granted the products of its operations as "self-evident," so that the *who* we are and the *where* we are and the *context* in which we are, present themselves as manifestly obvious — as *apparently* irreducible givens—as immanent, firmly implanted, irreducible features of us.

Yet we are, all the while, enmeshed in psyche. We owe our experiential basis to it, even as it never directly reveals its *own* existence and location to us, where and how it resides vis-à-vis where and how *we* experience ourselves to be. Indeed, the reality it so seamlessly assembles for us places us (during wakeful states, for instance) in our outer world settings as *artifacts* of the reality it creates around us. Similarly, the psyche places us within the context of our dream reality(ies)—assembling these alternate settings even as it projects us into them. In neither situation—wakeful reality or dream reality—is the psyche's existence ever revealed as separate, or removed, or independent, or a priori, in terms of either time or space. Hence its transparency.

Perhaps postulating the psyche as the unseen organ of perception and assembler of reality—the seat of consciousness—may seem an outlandish construct. On the other hand, the eye, by way of analogy, develops and functions perfectly well without ever directly seeing itself. As an "object" it is transparent to its own function, never focused upon itself despite its profound, functional capacity to gather light and focus. It can't, unaided, observe itself. Encouraged by this analogy, perhaps our notion about the psyche isn't so off-the-wall, after all. So let's continue with it!

If the psyche receives the impressions of any and all inputs, and assembles our various subjective

The Ground of Knowing

(sleeping and wakeful, concrete or abstract) realities at all times and in all places (ever constructing for us our experience, moment to moment, of time and place), then psyche ever surrounds us even as we ever reside within it. Its transparency makes it appear (if we dwell on it) that psyche "comes to us" wherever "we" are, but the relative truth may be that we are always within *it*, wherever *it* is, and all our apparent realities (including even our neurology) are its constructs of *us*. Our experiences may only be apparently "outer" or "inner"—indeed quite possibly we never really go "anywhere" (being, instead "nowhere" or "*now* *here*"). In such an arrangement it is the remarkable quality of the psyche's convincing assembly job which provides us the illusion of our realities as we encounter and traverse them within our exterior/material and interior/mental perceptions of space and time, along with the contexts in which these perceptions are placed— either "wakefulness" and/or "dream."

So, to return to my original question: What, then, if everything is "psychic"—of the psyche?

One possibility that follows is that the psyche exists independently of our apparent space-time/material-mental/awake-dreaming constitutions, since presumably the latter (collectively) depend upon the former for our even being able to be aware of them, while the former exists apparently a priori—perhaps comprising the very ground of being itself.

The relative, convincing context and quality of our material reality would, then, presumably have as much to do with the *stridency* of the input material reaching the psyche from any and all sources, as it would with the specific content of the raw sensory data itself.

In other words, the psyche always "attends"—is in attentional mode. It's always "on," registering whatever is reaching it, from whatever source, and assembling from that whatever reality we experience. Perhaps psyche is a bit like a "drop-stuff/stuffit-expander" program in a computer. Densely packed data streams are dropped into it and the psyche performs operations on this input, unbundling it into a workable, explicated environment. It may be doing something akin to this constantly.

How does the tenor and stridency of the material—the input—impressing itself upon the psyche get triaged? How does the psyche "know" what input to attend to and take into account, and what to disregard or ignore? Perhaps the whole notion of "intensity" or stridency or loudness (however imprecise the terms) constitutes one category of triage. And what typically has the greatest immediate intensity—the most "loudness"—is the data arising from our sensorium—our bodies. In wakeful consciousness we are immersed in (or inundated with) what we refer to as our "senses"—touch, taste, smell, hearing, feeling, sight—all the stimulation appearing to arise in the outer world—as well as all the proprioception (sensory impressions arising from stimuli sourced within the body itself rather than spurred only by external stimuli). Add to this our intuitional stream (and

The Ground of Knowing

probably any number of other "byte-streams" arising within) during every moment of wakeful life, and we — our psyches (or our psyches, and therefore "we," via our psyches) — are utterly saturated, drenched in input. This input, collectively, is the "loudest." Any more extensive starscape remains blotted out, so to speak, during the brightness of the sunlit hours. "High noon" is always loud and local, while dimmer and subtler contrasts (whatever intimations or potentials they contain) may appear as no more than traces of the trackless.

Therefore, because it is the loudest, collective source of input bearing in upon the psyche, the psyche draws on the bitstream of the body-sensorium, and fashions for us our most compelling and apparently consistent reality — one to which we attach our first name as a moniker of personal identity, and one in which we encounter and live out our perception of self as an incarnate, separate, individual and indivisible person. This reality, the product of psyche's work upon the collective data-stream of the sensorium, is immediate, immanent and recurring — moment by moment, day by day, year by year. Indeed, psyche assembles and generates (flashes back to us) all the tethers and referents — people, places, things, events, circumstances, situations, environments, institutions — which confer upon us this reality: the reality of the personal "I" and the "I's" lifetime — its constancy as well as its flow.

If psyche is ever-present and a priori, and if

it generates who we experience ourselves to be within a context, then it is reasonable to pose the following questions. What *other* data streams reach the psyche—make an impression upon it—in addition to the body-sensorium, and what are the realities (and our own identities within these realities) that arise from psyche's orchestration of these other streams of input? Additionally, do other streams of input, sourced elsewhere, ever get orchestrated into the reality of the bodily sensorium, coloring it or "flavoring" it—and our personal identity within it—in any discernible way during our wakeful, body-centered hours?

The "dream" reality gives us a clue about this. During sleep the body-sensorium's data stream is greatly reduced. For example, relative paralysis of limbs is one of the features of sleeping. Most (though admittedly not all) data as might arise from the sensory encounter with external/outerworld stimuli is markedly lowered as input to the psyche. The data stream orchestrated into our material reality, so loud and local during "wakeful" hours, recedes. The psyche, however, never sleeps and is still as active as ever, continuing to explicate whatever reaches it.

Perhaps it is from the phenomena involved with what might generically be called "sensory-deprivation" experiences that the traces of the autonomous psyche are most apparent to us, if we stop to reflect on them. Of course, such a condition ("sensory deprivation") is a bit of a misnomer, because the psyche is *always* awash in streams of input and is not sensory-deprived at all! From the psyche's own vantage point, the muting of the data-stream stemming from the body-sensorium (as this routinely arises within our sleeping reality on Mother Earth) is simply the cessation of *one* input. The psyche's iris, so to speak, immediately adapts to this cessation, dilating its pupil, widening the receptive sphere to gather, amplify and incorporate the remaining, lower "volume," less loud (less bright) sensory starscape, in all its infiniteness, into the reality-making mix.

Within the "sleep" (dream) reality, we become aware of extraordinary constructions of a multi-tiered nature going on, much of which appears to have no stake in tethering itself to our assumed frames of reference — time, space, sequence, personal identity, the body — as we routinely experience them in the wakeful state.

The input being fashioned into these weird (to our way of sense-making) or off-beat, even bizarre or sublime realities is of much lower loudness than that supplied through the body-sensorium — but it is *much* more extensive.

Other relative sensory-deprivation (again with qualified apology for the use of this expression) environments — the floating/weightless environment of a sensory-deprivation isolation tank, for instance, and the "quieting the mind" regimens inherent in many meditational disciplines — also seem conducive to revealing the starscape of the mind once the sun of focused intensity is shaded. And the results of such experiences are powerfully suggestive that the psyche has no shortage of input during such times, and continues to be actively engaged in reality-construction during them.

Anecdotal reports arising from near-death experiences also support the presence of a rich variety of reality-promulgating input reaching the psyche, and rich reality-constructions emanating from it, in the absence of the usual input from the body-sensorium.

So what if we—each of us—resides, in essence (essentially), "in psyche" rather than "in-body"—notwithstanding that we experience ourselves and our personal identity as being in-body—i.e., embodied, *literally in the body*?

What if these eyes—looking out on an early Saturday morning over a carpet of sprinkler-soaked lawn, as a gentle breeze kisses this face, observe this scene not merely from the depths of eye sockets, but from the depths of psyche—standing outside of time, of space, even of personal identity—registering and assembling this scene even as psyche places "me" within it?

Can I feel the presence of "psyche"—the home base of cognition, the seat of consciousness—notwithstanding (or in spite of) its transparency and liminal qualities? Can I experience the current scene—and a million prior settings as well as all future ones—as being taken up within the psyche, as was the quill ink by the blotters on the hardwood desks of the pre-ballpoint pen school days of my childhood?

The Ground of Knowing

If I reside in psyche, then *in some measure I continue to be fashioned within psyche in the absence of the data stream of the body-sensorium*. My personal identity may or may not carry over, but the essential "I"—the fundaments—which include the underpinnings of personal identity—my psyche's capacity to assemble and express itself as embodied "personal identity" (which is of psyche itself)—inalienably is.

To develop a *sensing* of psyche, a feeling for its transparency in which psyche's liminal qualities come to be *felt* as evidence of its very existence—to see all experience as concentric to the psyche as silent-but-ever-present partner, the ever-living reality of my foundation—to have the intimation that there are *always* data streams being assembled—is to find oneself immersed in the timeless, the eternal, of every apparently present and ephemeral moment.

Within such (an) experience—that of sensing the concentricity of psyche within each moment—lies the experience of "pure being." Is it I who experiences pure being as part of who "I" am within psyche?... Or am I living out and experiencing a version of Psyche's own experience of itself, quite apart from its function of being impressed upon and assembling? The distinction may be meaningless. For within the simultaneous experience of the concentricity of psyche and me, of psyche and every present wakeful (and sleep-full) moment, the transpersonal home base beyond personal identity, body sensorium, and psychical function simply *is*. Underlying, overlaying, assembling, witnessing, recording, ever in quiet repose, more trackless than the whole breadth and depth of what we think we know or can imagine, Psyche, the hearth of consciousness, is ever within us, ever in, through and about us—perfusing us completely. The organ of perception is redolent in its seamless creation and carrying of us.

The Extensions of Consciousness

In our day-in, day-out reality most of us would report (were we asked to stop, consider and do so) that our consciousness—our awareness—the center of our being, resides in our heads, somewhere behind the eyes and between the ears. This is where we—our awareness—seem to live as we take in, peruse and assess. We are "in here." Indeed, even when the body is wounded—say in the case of a stubbed toe—we typically appraise such a physical insult as if from a distance, reconnoitering its ache as if it is "out there" while we remain, objectively, in the head—"in here." Injury may bring us up short and remind us that we are embodied, but injury to the body does not necessarily change the locus of where we experience our centrality of consciousness to reside.

It may even be axiomatic that bodily injury, or perhaps infirmity of any sort, fosters the perception of head-as-the-home-base-of-awareness. There is always, apparently, the safe, recessed, retreated, encased refuge from which to assess and respond to what is "out there."

Yet the actual reality is that the experience of the "home-base" of consciousness is utterly malleable.

Who's At Home In Your Body (When You're Not)?

The sense of home-based-ness can augment and diminish, expand and contract in direct proportion to consciousness's function-of-the-moment. We are typically so absorbed in whatever the function of consciousness is, within any given moment, that we aren't thinking in terms of the coordinates which would delineate the seat of its (our) apparent residence.

For instance, imagine yourself riding a bicycle, and in this instance having a thorough familiarity with the bike. Familiarity means that you (and your body) are completely kinesthetically attuned to the experience of riding this particular bike. You *know* this experience intimately — the tensing and flexing of the frame, the resistance, cadence and torque range any set of gear ratios between the front sprocket and the rear sprocket will engender on the pedal cranks, the varying effects on riding that any combination of terrain, wind and surface will have, and so on. Now pretend, as a thought experiment (or if you have a bike, think up a challenging ride and try this), that you are taking a fairly swift ride with bursts of downhill acceleration accompanying a twisting, narrow course. What happens, during such a ride, to the seat of consciousness?

Simply this: the seat of consciousness no longer resides in the head as "in here." The seat of consciousness expands to *include the entire experience* — especially the feel and capabilities of the bike combined with you, the rider. In other words, consciousness "e-x-t-e-n-d-s" to take into itself the attributes of the bike as if they were/are its *own* immediate capabilities — even

The Extensions of Consciousness

as if the bicycle itself is now become a seamless extension of both body and mind. This extension of consciousness is all-inclusive of the experience. The bite, or traction, of tire-treads spraying gravel around a curve as bike and rider lean inwards as a single unit, offsetting the centrifugal force with its own centripetal force, the texture and sounds and strains of the bike frame, the torquing of the pedal cranks as extensions of flexing calves and haunches, the chatter of brake calipers as brake shoes nudge the wheel-rims, the wind—both the wind in your face and the cross gusts affecting the bike's attitude as they sporadically burst across your path—all this and more in attuned, exquisite, conscious participation becomes, in such a fluid moment, consciousness's new "home," *inseparable from its function. There is no longer an "in here" behind the eyes: there is, rather, a consciousness tweaked into a larger orb by its very extensions, intermingling with an "out there" which, though still immense, is being more engaged and appropriated through consciousness's own expansion via its extensions.*

In such a moment (and these are what moments are), personal consciousness expands beyond personal identity to become synonymous with what we're doing—i.e., being and doing are one.

The possibility of this extension of consciousness is tacitly acknowledged in our everyday use of language. There are, for example, certain nouns which are simultaneously either verbs or adjectives, as if the "thing" is best designated by a term characterizing what it does, or how it is observed to act or behave, or as some quality which it exemplifies. The most obvious example of this is "fly" — in this case a word designating an insect best known by its attribute of pure flight — or (perhaps) a kind of pure flight best exemplified by this insect. Another example is the word "slide," which denotes both a thing characterized by "sliding" motion (regardless of whether the thing is an inanimate, rigid playground structure or a stripped bare swath down a mountainside), or, on the other hand, sliding motion characterized by a thing. "Swing" is a similar example. So is "jerk." Noun/adjective overlaps, in which a thing is inseparable from a quality attributed to it, are also quite common, as in "swift," the name of a bird, and "orange."

So what is pure human "doing?" Where, and to what, do our extensions of consciousness lead us? If the locus of consciousness constantly recalibrates to encompass the maxima and the minima of that to which it attends, if the "in here" and the "out there" are never not in flux, then, perchance, human being-ness — "being" (another thing or quality actually rooted in a verb presented in gerund form) — is as diaphanous as a wisp of smoke?

And if we really start to consider the human "being" in the light of extensions of consciousness, may we not, as we putter about, start to nudge across, at some point, a conceptual boundary in which we come to realize that what we are perusing is less about human being-ness and more about just "plain-vanilla" consciousness?

The Extensions of Consciousness

When our consciousness experiences itself as synonymous with its extensions and recalibrates itself to them—when the local seat of consciousness calibrates its apparent size and place to suit/fit its apparent function of the moment—either while riding a bicycle (as well as through absorption into any outer-world activity), or passively "observing" the most distant galaxy through its extensions (as observing through a telescope), or "extending" inwards ("intending"?) via ultrasound, meditation or any other means—*our consciousness has, beyond any given moment, no fixed abode or home*. Within the immediacy of any such moments, are we any less immersed in the immensity of that moment's experience than is, say, a dragonfly-on-the-wing, skimming a pond surface or riding the air currents? Are we any other (any "thing" other) than immersed in and transfixed by that to which our consciousness is calibrated? Is our consciousness's participation in reality (whatever that means) of any different order than that of a tree's consciousness now become sensate to the sun's warmth penetrating its bark or a person's arms squeezing the girth of its circumference, or a cumulonimbus thunderhead's consciousness now billowing awake through its own tension, swelling and discharge?

Our human consciousness, moving from "in-the-head" (behind the eyes and between the ears), where it resides only while in one particular mode of assessing, *becomes* participatory consciousness of which the strongest feature is not "human" consciousness at all, but the fact that it is *participatory*, i.e., in the sway of that which transfixes it, no longer knowable as residing anywhere, only knowable by the scope of its involvement and enthrallment. At this level all consciousnesses—that of the bicyclist, the tree, the swift, the orange, the celestial gazer, the meditator, the dragonfly, the thunderhead—are functionally identical.

If the encasement of personal consciousness is such an illusion—if our true home of consciousness is as malleable and diaphanous as even the most commonplace experiences, upon reflection, lead us to conclude—then whatever "our" consciousness is, is capable of overlapping and even merging—finding harmony, dissonance, melody, syncopation, rhythm, orchestration—with all other consciousnesses that encounter us, even as these other consciousnesses calibrate *their* own "self"-ness to include us in their experience—taking each one of us as a part of their altered home-base—i.e., as an extension of *them*. With consciousness there is only this dance. Personal, embodied selfhood—consciousness "in the head"—is only as tangible (and as lifeless) as a frozen moment's snapshot thumbtacked to a wall, or a chloroformed moth impaled under glass.

We can therefore infer that consciousness is tantamount to relatedness—that we can only "know" something concurrent with that something's knowing of us—and this is true whether what we seek to know is another person, or a gust of wind.

As an experienced reality, this inviolable, ineluctable

The Extensions of Consciousness

truth has the power to awaken—and alter—attitude. And a change in attitude has the power to be a redefinition of who we experience ourselves to be. Such a deep implication to arise through following the course of consciousness's "extensions!"

By this measure, there is no privacy, no hiddenness. Everything is fluid and available to be known in some fashion. Bodily encased (cranially encased) personal identity is a special-case-only form of consciousness—but one no more or less special than any other of consciousness's flexations. The recognition that, as we follow the course of consciousness's extensions, we enter, experientially, into a realm of *generic* consciousness—no longer explicitly "human" consciousness at all, but, rather, a *field* of consciousness—one created, held and experienced in common by all living things—by all consciousness—can be the discovery of an ancient, yet vitally alive kinship existing between us and all other levels, places, activities, and time-frames of being.

Perhaps, most interestingly, this new (or is it very old?) awareness is *not* a leap in consciousness. *It is itself, rather, an incremental extension grounded in utterly unexceptional events*. It is, as well, an awakening to the pervasiveness of the ebbing and flowing of consciousness's boundaries—of the interpenetrating and knowing-relatedness unavoidably encountered at every turn—at every level of being... And the recursive enrichment that this awakening stirs in us—*that* is the real story.

Who's At Home In Your Body (When You're Not)?

The Consciousness of Intimacy

The consciousness of intimacy is that consciousness which arises between two (or more) people when (and as) they, either sequentially or concurrently, reveal their deepest vulnerabilities to one another.

This experience of peering into the vulnerability of another—and of permitting another to peer, unobstructed, into the depths of one's own soul—is nowhere more exactingly enacted than during the course of sexual intercourse/expression between two in-love partners en route to, and including, orgasmic climax. This is not the only avenue through which vulnerability can be observed and revealed, but it may be the most recurrent of all like experiences.

The consciousness of intimacy, then, invokes two basic components. The first (listed in arbitrary order) is the act of observing the voluntarily revealed vulnerability of another; the second is the open revealing of—the inviting in of the other person as observer to—one's own recess of personal torment and ecstasy. In the most moving of all shared intimacies, both the observation and the revelation occur simultaneously between both partners.

Who's At Home In Your Body (When You're Not)?

Observing as an intimate act

Within sexual expression, soul contact is most discernibly established when one partner (whom we shall designate as the "lover," in this example), if invited, by whatever means, to do so,[1] looks into the eyes of the other—in this case, the one to receive succor (whom we shall term the "beloved").

What may commence as an invitation-by-gesture can become an imploring—beseeching—invitation to look ever more deeply into the eyes of the beloved as he or she becomes more sexually aroused. This *always* evokes a concurrent emotional tenor in both partners. From the observational standpoint, looking into the eyes—meeting the eye and holding the gaze—of the increasingly aroused beloved evokes a feeling of wonder in the lover to be invited in and allowed to observe in such close proximity the other's soul. This utter lack of pretense and defensiveness—this utter opening of the soul vehicle to the perusal and probing of the lover—is very, very moving.

As the gaze between the two partners locks, there is the sense of the lover's being drawn into the beloved at unprecedented depth, almost as if both bodies and both souls are somehow one. Within such a met gaze there is literally "nowhere to run, nowhere to hide."

---

1) In the situation of one or both partners being unsighted, or sighted partners making love in an unlit space, equivalent sensory exchanges are possible in establishing pristine, unfettered intimate connection.

The Consciousness of Intimacy

And yet (as this discursiveness is fashioned as if the orgasms between the two partners are sequential) the lover's consciousness usually takes the side of caring for and nourishing and providing for the one who is so vulnerable—so without affectation in the sexual act. The lover is often overwhelmed with a flood of compassion for the aroused beloved, with a degree of unconditional, fully present love and attentiveness that overflows into intense compassionate succor for the now fully aroused partner.

If the *lover/provider's* experience were to translate into first-person commentary, it might go something like this:

"I see you so completely open to me, inviting me in with no barriers, no resistance—and as I peer ever so deeply into your inviting eyes they become transparent to me and I find myself looking past their (your) crystalline lenses and mosaiced irises into the internal canopy of your soul. And there I discover, in its rhythmic and insistent rising and falling, everywhere you—your soul—has ever been and all the times it has ever cried out for completeness—for being made whole. I am aware of entering freely into that sanctum you have opened for me, and as you crescendo into orgasm I see your creaturehood and your divinity all mushed together—the body transporting you beyond here and now—your soul-gaze taking leave of the body and, no longer looking through the eyes, becoming aligned with the procreative pulse of the Universe, carrying over that primordial swelling and splitting into a timeless, spaceless eternal moment.

"This I witness at such close range as to lose track of myself as an observer—an invited guest. I experience myself more as having become a celebrant in a cosmic sacrament—a worshipper of celestial ooze. To know you at such stunning depth is to have my own capacity for depth revealed to me. To know you at this stunning depth is to know that you and I have always been communing at depth—so entwined—throughout eternity. To know you at this depth is to know that you and I live out our own participation in this eternal, universal dance passably well."

"Inviting In" as an Intimate act

The consciousness of intimacy is altogether unique from the standpoint of "inviting another in" to the inner sanctum of one's own soul as a structural ingredient of sexual expression—of making love. The eyes open wide and seek to engage the other—the lover—who is rousing the beloved. As this gaze is met, the sense of *inclusion* is profound. The lover is invited in, to peer into the beloved's eyes—unobstructed—and the lover is free to discover whatever resides within them, through them and behind them. The beloved has no reservations about anything the lover might observe. Whatever, there, is…, simply is.

The beloved's gaze is heightened by the raised level of arousal coursing through as the lover "learns me." As the aroused's gaze holds, met by the lover, all resistance to the body's elevating pitch of pleasure—any possible

The Consciousness of Intimacy

self-consciousness or embarrassment regarding the involuntary, spontaneous issuance of grunts, groans, strains, grimaces—completely ceases. The beloved is now a throbbing, pulsing mass into the interstices of which the lover gazes, enters and takes up residence—and the beloved, already thrilled to be opening the entrance—entered by the lover—is enthralled to be now so thoroughly explored and so completely known. As the beloved rises towards orgasm, his/her soul in all its plight is boldly visible—daring to be seen—and, yes, daring the other to see it. To be so completely known and loved and succored in such a fluid present recalibrates the connectedness of the beloved's whole being in a symphony of rapture. The lover's eyes and gaze, so fully answering the imploring of the beloved to be searched and known to the very depths, are now within the beloved always.

If the experience of the beloved (the one observed) were to be verbally expressed to the lover (the observer), they might be something like this:

"I see you, and I am potentially self-conscious about how I look and the sounds that I'm starting to make, involuntary movements of my body, and the expressions, grimacing or otherwise, that may overtake me. Yet I invite you in through my eyes for I need to be known—and I need *you* to know me. And you take me up on my invitation—how amazing! The touch of your gaze, at my behest, enters me. I feel it. The stridency of the rising cadence of my breath and the tethered tenor of my loins is now, as our eyes lock, my gift to you, in response to your loving succor of me. Your expression, so earnest and encouraging, disarms me. You are my partner in the cosmic dance of life, with all its destructive and procreative potential—unerringly present to me now—with me in my moment of ecstasy, inseparable from it.

"I'm coming now, and I hear myself announcing to you that I am. Through the chords and strains of inner bliss I allow you—your caress and your gaze—to possess me utterly. I am the one you love. Know me. You have always known me. I meet God this way and we meet God this way and you are my priest, my consort, my witness, my confessor. I subside, basking in the sublimity of a boundaryless knowing, the joy of having been known (and being known) for my innermost heart."

✧ ✧ ✧

In the aforementioned example of intimacy-consciousness, the arena of sexual expression between two in-love individuals was drawn upon because the experience of sexual bliss is sublime enough to be transporting while recurring often enough to be widely replicable (should any of my readers want to explore extending the boundaries of their own intimacy-consciousness).

It should be noted, however, that the use of the sexual arena for this purpose is *didactic*. The elements of observing—being drawn into—the vulnerability

The Consciousness of Intimacy

of another, and conversely (and sometimes simultaneously), the need to be *known* within one's own vulnerability and the drawing upon another to enter and witness it—the two defining elements of the consciousness of intimacy—can arise and be present in many other settings. These include, and are not limited to: tending-to-another (or being-tended-to) in the wake of an accident or during an illness (especially life-threatening or terminal illness); the experience of pulling together as community in the wake of natural disaster or unnatural calamity (in which there are abundances of openly expressed need and spontaneous, anonymous acts of kindness, assistance and compassion); that which passes, sometimes, between friends as they live out, and witness, the joys and sorrows of life's unfolding tapestry in and between each other; sudden, "chance" encounters in which an exchange occurs stemming from the awakening of an unanticipated "connection" with another; artistic expression (in any area) which may raise strong evocative potential between creator and observer; acts of generosity which forge a link between "ready-to-be-known-as-having-a-need-to-receive" and "ready-to-be-known-for-having-a-need-to-give"; as well as in all settings that evoke strong empathic connection between people, and settings in which the human dynamic of parent/child (whether involving one's actual parents or children, or equivalent roles such as mentoring/being mentored) is activated.

Perhaps the dropping of pretense—the "letting

one's hair down," in which the common ground of being (of our shared humanity) gets revealed and removes, at least temporarily, the distinctions of gender and gender preference, race, creed, ethnicity, class, generation—the supposedly insurmountable barriers which routinely segregate and partition us from one another on the basis of our "uniqueness," elitism (of any stripe) and unexamined self-righteousness during most of our wakeful hours—is the essence of the passing through the portal into the consciousness of intimacy.

The Visual Play of Consciousness

The visual field is a playground of consciousness. The actual "field" of the visual field is immense. If you sit up against a tree and focus straight ahead while extending your arms straight out on either side of your body so that they are 180 degrees to one another (forming a straight line from the fingertips of one hand to the fingertips of the other), and then, *while continuing to focus straight ahead*, move ever so slightly forward the outstretched arms and hands until they just become discernible within the visual field, and then check where the arms actually are vis-à-vis the torso, you'll be surprised (I think) to see the arms not much shy of 180 degrees to one another! So the lateral plane of the visual field sweeps out an arc of nearly 180 degrees.

If you then lie upon the grass in an open field or in the middle of a large swath of freshly mowed lawn, with your eyes directed straight up overhead—finding a point to focus on there (a portion of a cloud, perhaps), and then see what is detectable at the edges of the peripheral field while you hold your vertical gaze—you'll notice again that the lateral field is about 180 degrees, and the head-to-toe field (the vertical plane if you were standing) is about 120 degrees or so. So the visual field, encompassing the focal plane and the periphery, comprises really the better part of a hemisphere—a veritable canopy of spatial perception.

Exploring a bit our experience with the visual field, we are able to discover some tantalizing analogues to the structure of consciousness. (Vision certainly lends itself to such analogues—and even *must* lend itself—for it is, after all, one modality through which consciousness gets to express, and experience, itself in our four-dimensional, space-time world.)

We might begin by drawing just the most obvious analogy between the focal point of consciousness within the visual field—that "spot" where we appear to be able to see most clearly—and ego consciousness. That spot which "we" are looking at—that spot of clearest articulation—*that* spot is the object not only of visual attention, but of conscious *intention*, as well. This artifact of vision is the spot with which we are, within any given daily moment, most immediately concerned. "I"-ness—the directed will—ego consciousness, controls the aiming of this plane of detailed vision, in accordance with conscious (ego) imperative. The focal point—that point on the focal plane within the overall visual field—both highlights what "directed will" seeks to fathom, as well as the existence of "directed will" itself. As a point of focus constituting an analogue to ego-consciousness—to "I"-ness—this aspect of vision, is both "what we're looking at"—intending to see, and ego-consciousness as the "I" who is doing the

The Visual Play of Consciousness

aiming and focusing.

Yet do note that within nearly all of the volume of the hemisphere of sensation and perception which the visual field *is*, that which we appear to see most "clearly"—the object of our focus—comprises, at any moment, only a puny little locus within this immensity of the entire visual field. The attempt can be made to make the focal point dart around, in rapid succession, to sample various "spots" within a previously held visual field, either by moving the entire head (unavoidably shifting the entire orientation of the visual hemisphere each time it moves), or by motions of the eyeballs only (while keeping the head stationary), but the endeavor to grasp-by-focus—to capture the contents of the more extended visual field by bringing them, piecemeal, into sharp, visual/conscious focus is, beyond a certain point, a prohibitively exhausting activity, and quickly reveals itself as a futile quest.

The analogue with ego-consciousness, I trust, is not lost. If one tries to encompass the field of life-experience by forcing each part of it into a relational assessment under the purview of the "personal I (eye)"—the ego—life will exhaust us long before it has yielded much to headlong—and headstrong—intention.

It's also worth noting, by way of analogy to consciousness, that our visual field always has a "blind spot" in it—a morphological imperative, apparently, for the site where the optic nerve joins the back of the eyeball results in a small area on the interior of each eye upon which the image passing through the retina cannot find focus. The rod and cone cell receptors are displaced by the joining of the optic nerve itself. So a blind spot is a "given," at all times, to being "sighted." We are not typically aware of our blind spot because the optic nerve for each eye does not join the eyeball directly along the focal plane (which establishes its focus in a region of the retina called the fovea), but, rather, at corresponding off focal-axis points within the peripheral field. Additionally, our perceptual system patches together—invents or creates, if you will, in a process called visual processing—a patterned filling which essentially blinds us to the existence of our blind spot. This patterned filling is an extension of whatever the play of vision is, in the immediate vicinity of the blind spot. One might say that the blind spot is filled with that which most conforms to whatever vision is adjacent to it—that it is filled with whatever "one would assume one is most likely to see" there.

The analogy to consciousness is quite obvious here. Conscious clarity always has its blindness—in *both* aspects: its actual inability to "see" clearly (comprehensively), and *its subjective blindness to its own inability to see clearly (comprehensively)*. There is always *something* of which consciousness is unaware—something not being seen—and consciousness is usually unaware of that which eludes it because consciousness unconsciously fills in a void of knowing with "what it expects to see there."

Incidentally, this tendency to "fill in the blank," even in instances not directly connected to the morphology of the blind spot, and its attendant inferences for understanding aspects of consciousness, can be very dramatically demonstrated. Two instances of this come to mind. The first involves an activity which my peers and I refer to as "walking rail." The second peruses, by way of anecdote, a condition known as "vitreous floaters." Let's consider "walking rail" first.

If you "walk rail"—if you walk along railroad tracks, between the two rails, and maintain a soft gaze straight ahead of you as you course along a straight section of track—at some point the rails will apparently disappear! (Please note: *If* you try this, choose an old or abandoned rail-bed and *always* have someone else with you who is the designated train-spotter—just in case. "Walking rail" can be *very* hypnotic, and it is possible to be in such an entranced state as to not notice even a very slow-moving train approaching you head-on![1] The analogy to consciousness is that consciousness is easily "entrained" (pun intended) and starts to sample and assemble reality very differently as it falls under the spell of repetitive stimulus (in this case, perchance, the strobe effect of the railroad ties passing beneath ones feet in the lower periphery of the visual field). Under

---

1) I write from experience: On one occasion, in Wellesley, Massachusetts, as I was transfixed in "walking rail," a slow-moving freight train was backing up towards me, approaching me from the very direction towards which I was walking. I would have walked right into it, and ended up a stain on the roadbed, had not my dear friend Charles Quinlan, in a steady voice (with no more than ten seconds to spare) alerted me. I owe Charlie my life.

these conditions vision becomes less discriminating and more prone to conjuring, without necessarily realizing, or making an announcement about, its own alteration.

Visual processing, in this example, creates an impression of visual cohesiveness and homogeneity that, lacking the discordance of other compelling sensory input, we would never suspect of being fraudulent—or at least tendentious. The cognitive dissonance of "knowing" that you're walking along a set of railroad tracks, feeling your shifts of balance as railroad ties pass irregularly under your feet—while losing the visual confirmation that you are walking along railroad track—notwithstanding that the eyes are still open and "seeing"—can be very disconcerting. "Vision," in this instance, is not "filling in" a gap in information. It is, rather, through entrainment via a stroboscopic effect, being lulled into rejecting essential information. One analogy to consciousness (among any number of others) is that consciousness can be "lulled" into suspending the acuity of its function—succumbing, in a way, and fostering in the mind it serves, an uncritical acceptance of a truly deficiently represented reality. *Caveat viditor*! ("Let the seer beware!")

Regarding the workings of neurological processing in the presence of an ocular condition called vitreous floaters, and the analogies this neurological processing suggests regarding human consciousness, generally, here is a personal reminiscence.

The Visual Play of Consciousness

I have had the condition known as vitreous floaters since the age of five. I first noticed this condition while on vacation at Brewster, on Cape Cod, in the early 1950s. My parents had taken my brother and me to one of the glacial kettle ponds that are strung across sections of Cape Cod—remnants of the last ice age. The water in the ponds is as clear and clean as freshly buffed lead crystal glass.

On that afternoon long ago, as I looked up to the sky I was surprised to notice what looked like a short, squiggly line, about the width of a road as depicted on a travel map, and including, at one end, a small circle, again like a town or village marker on such a map. Indeed, this was how I described it to my disinterested parents. I noticed how the little two-sided line—a bit curved—and its associated unfilled-in circular "dit," were "floating" before my eyes. I kind of knew that it wasn't "in the sky," but, as a five-year old lacking the diagnostic or conceptual abilities to more accurately describe this phenomenon, I let the matter go with my parents. However it continued to intrigue me. What was I doing with a segment of road map in my eye?

Vitreous floaters, a condition attributed to a thickening of the vitreous fluid (or gel) in which congealed cellular bunches start to precipitate out of the normally clear ocular medium, have been with me ever since. And they have increased markedly, especially in more recent times (as I approach my sixties). However, even thirty years ago (some twenty-three years after the initial discovery), I would occasionally find myself swatting at a fly that wasn't there, or playing psychedelic games with myself while in a chandeliered room (the living room at the Boston Center for Adult Education was one of my favorites for this). While sitting under a chandeliered ceiling, I could, with a quick flick of my head, "stir them up"—a bit like the encapsulated ivory snow-flake snowstorm of a liquid-encased, globular winter scene—and then rest, observing the floaters as they worked their way down through the jewelled-like cut-glass cacophony of chandeliered lights. As the floaters would pass before ("through") the multi-mirrored light bulbs in the chandelier, and their related glass reflectors, the optical effects of my floaters would further scatter the light in semi-halo-fashion (sometimes obscuring the local light source altogether) as they would "snow down" through the chandeliers. I must have looked strange, to those who might have noticed, as I gave occasional "head flicks" for, outwardly, no apparent reason. However, this was one way I "played with me," turning an annoyance into a fascination.

Across decades, the floater situation has worsened considerably. At this point in my life I view the world through a never-ending procession—almost a phantasmagoria—of roadmaps, with their countless highways and byways, replete with designations of villages, cities and towns, urban sprawl, redundant highways—an insane network, indeed, were it ever to be rendered into concrete and asphalt—a madman's traffic grid!

The Visual Play of Consciousness

I view my world through this tangle. However, any time I want "clear vision," I need but pause and momentarily be still—not even to the extent of gazing, just momentarily easing off of moving my eyes around from one point of focus to another—and the miraculous neurological processing, just cited (sighted?) in the "walking rail" example, "insinuates itself" into this crisscrossed, pretzelated scene. To wit: to all appearances—literally—the neurological process constituting vision nulls out completely from my field of view the altering effects of severe vitreous floaters. While I am still, my vision is as clear as a windless pond surface, and my visual field, to all appearances, has nothing interposing itself from within that comes between me and my visually tactile experience of the world.

A slight jiggle of my head and... it's all back!... but within even a moment's hesitation the nulling, filtering, processing capabilities of my visual neurology start to impose themselves, unbidden. It is really quite miraculous.

So here are further analogies, stemming from my vitreous floaters condition, to more general human consciousness. There are really two possible inferences as to the functioning of consciousness that may be implied by these experiences I have reported. These inferences could not be more dissimilar and I don't know which is more "right," or at least less wrong.

The first inference is a hopeful one: If, amidst a "confusion" of any sort—cognitive, mental, emotional, spiritual, etc.—one can find a "place" of quiet, or "stillness," it is possible that the reality one is truly encountering will become "clear," and the outlines of "what is really there" will become discernible. This lesson, then, is, "Stillness clarifies."

The second inference, however, is quite different. In the second inference we are forced to acknowledge, based on this analysis, that *"clarity" is always suspect*. Even though my remarkable neurological processing filters out, in those quieter moments, the "distractions" from what I *want* to be seeing (rendering them, in the moment, "invisible"), they are, nonetheless, still there. Clarity, seen this way, is always "apparent," or partial. Clarity of vision—the "knowing" of what's "really" out there—is so seductive because it *seems* so complete. It seeks not, nor feels any need, to gather cognitions beyond its own relatively "clear" vantage point. It is frozen beauty—*not in motion*. Yet the reality, though screened from knowing-in-the-moment—screened from consciousness—is still there, with its greater complexity and messiness. The perfectly balanced equilibrium of visual chaos offset by neurological processing finds itself, with a moment's jerk of motion, instantly "disequilibriumed" with the addition of apparently new, random variables *that were never not there*, even though they were not, at the moment of clarity, "in the picture." In short, as seductive as clarity of vision—and, by analogy, clarity of conscious awareness—may appear, there is always the caution to not take undue refuge in what appears "certain."

The Visual Play of Consciousness

Indeed, the "distortions" that can muddy up a pristine vista, and mindscape, acknowledged or not, may be, as far as I can tell, ever present, with their locus and provenance not even discernible as residing either "in here" or "out there."

In concluding this section on vitreous floaters and their contribution to my understandings about both vision and consciousness, as I approach sixty years of age, I smile as I fathom this attempt at meaning-making, spurred on by an innocent quest inaugurated in the mind of a wonderful little tow-haired boy on a sunny, fine-grained beach by a Cape Cod pond well over a half-century ago. What started out as a solitary little dot of a town along some untrodden one-road backwater gradually morphed into the floater equivalent of megalopolis' urban sprawl running the length of the East Coast corridor—perhaps, ever more insistently, demanding my attention. (Now, dear Loving Spirit, having divined a bit of awareness regarding the relevance of some piece of this phenomena as it pertains to the structure of human consciousness, would you please let my floaters desist?)

✧ ✧ ✧

While perusing the subject of blind spots and fillings-in, I should note that "outside" and "beyond" the visual field—notwithstanding the blind spot within it—there resides within every moment more than a hemisphere's canopy of the unseen. Our near hemisphere of vision is immense, but it is, within any given moment and at all times, always eclipsed by the greater immensity of "the unseen"—the unseeable. We may infer what is contained within this unseen immensity via assuming, by way of extrapolation, that it is simply a continuation of what we actually see, drawing upon our other senses (such as hearing) which are not "blind" to input that arises from outside the visual field, but the limit on the faculty of vision appears absolute. In visual terms we are, in the aggregate, always more blind than sighted.

So let's recap, once again, some vision-inspired analogies to human consciousness. The analogues with consciousness are, I trust, straightforward:

(1) The "blind spots" within consciousness—those which, with effort, we're actually capable of seeing—are glossed over, or filled in, by that which we expect or want to see there, and only with considerable effort can we become aware that we provide the filling.

(2) Even conscious focus—the intention of consciousness to see something—can become entrained (entranced) into introducing distortions into what we think we're seeing, even while we believe ourselves to be aware with great clarity.

(3) Finally, any sphere of consciousness—of "knowing"—we evolve or attain is always eclipsed by the greater immensity not only of what is unknown, but also (the immensity) of what, in terms of focused consciousness, is inherently unknowable.

The Visual Play of Consciousness

☼ ☼ ☼

While we are on the topic of the visual field, I might, in passing, list a few other attributes of peripheral, *apparently* non-focused vision — the field (and expanse) of vision away from the focal plane. It was earlier noted that to try to assemble all that is contained within the peripheral field of view by darting the focal plane around it — either via abruptly shifting the eyes while holding the head steady (in which case there's not too much alteration in the visual field itself, i.e., in that which the visual field encompasses), or by holding the focus of the eyes relative to the head steady while moving orientation of the focal plane around via shifting the head (which also shifts, absolutely, the orientation of the visual field itself and therefore its contents) requires a prohibitive expenditure of energy. The entire visual system becomes quickly enervated under the load of this demand.

Given the immensity of the visual field exclusive of the focal plane/focal point, it is reasonable to wonder, "What is peripheral vision good for?" I would simply mention, in response, that there are kinds of seeing which peripheral vision is exquisitely suited to: it is adept at rendering, and bringing to conscious (or unconscious/autonomic) intention and mobilization, the new or changing *motion* of anything within its scope. It is equally exquisite in providing a sense of proportion/spatial relationship between and amongst all that is within the visual field, and it can play a role that is of more than passing importance in night vision. (The next time you walk an unlit wooded path after dark, rather than focus on the path itself, lift your gaze a bit above the path and see how the peripheral sphere of vision heightens contrast and "assembles" for you a more useful three-dimensional representation of the pathway ahead!)

Since we're using vision as a metaphor for consciousness in this chapter, let's examine a few implications of these more immediate examples.

The fact that motion is *especially* noticeable in the peripheral field brings us to a recognition: the motion that is sensed in this manner is not the result of visual focus, but is rather an alteration in the *pattern* of peripheral perception. If I'm sitting on the ground, leaning up against a tree and a person starts walking across my field of view, I notice this, first and foremost, as a disturbance or alteration in the pattern of my peripheral vision. I may quickly turn my head and bring the area of "disturbance" into alignment with the focal plane and resolve its image (and objectify, through focus, the "disturbance" into the image of a person), but the initial recognition is not one of focus; it is one of pattern alteration.

And it is just here that we realize that "conscious focus" and "visual focus" need not always be the same thing! In the example cited above, ***the disturbance in the peripheral field became an object of conscious focus — conscious attention — even while visual focus, and hence ego* consciousness, *were***

The Visual Play of Consciousness

directed elsewhere. That to which conscious focus was *subsequently* directed—that which drew to itself conscious focus—was, initially, only a blur: outside the purview of visual focus (and therefore disaligned[2] from the focal plane). So we start to gain something from this: in our everyday lives, our experience of visual focus and conscious focus are often synonymous (and focused vision is, as has already been mentioned, one analogy of ego consciousness: the "I" that looks out, with intention, on an "other"). Yet it now becomes apparent that observing, acute *conscious attentiveness can focus/be focused anywhere within the visual field—along the focal plane (its usual place) or anywhere else within the overall peripheral field itself!*—without changing the actual point of visual focus. Consciousness can be "acute and observing" even when that which is being observed is hazy, indistinct, fuzzy, murky or "out of focus."

A simple experience is illustrative of this. Find a nice tree to lean up against and have a seat by it. Find

---

2) While heretofore (according to the guardians of the English lexicon) not an official "word," "disalign" is hereby coined. It implies an *intentional* 'misalignment.' The sole use of the term "misalignment" implies more of an accidental happenstance—which, in this instance, would be misleading. It is wonderful that, as one of the increasing freedoms of advancing age, one can coin usage in any way that furthers the conveyance of meaning and sensibility, beyond caring much about the barks and snarls of stark censure by officious "keepers of the realm." Other neologisms and neo-coinisms occur throughout this, and my other books. Hopefully there aren't so many of them as to render my work hopelessly idiosyncratic.

Who's At Home In Your Body (When You're Not)?

a comfortable point to focus on, and look at it, making it (whatever it is) the object of your conscious attention and visual focus (the usual state of affairs). Now, let your visual focus "soften," slightly, into a gaze, without changing the visual focal point. Then, let your *conscious* focus—the focus of consciousness—start to "move around" within the visual field *without your changing the visual point of focus*. To some extent, you already had an experience of this earlier when you checked out the extensiveness of the visual field itself. In that instance you were focusing straight ahead while seeing where your "hands" became noticeable as you moved the arms forward. When you first actually noticed this, you weren't focusing on "hands." Rather, you noticed an alteration in the pattern of the perception of peripheral vision, and "knew" this alteration was your hands because you had set up the experiment. Now, however, while maintaining the soft focus on the point (whatever it is) in front of you, let your conscious attention—conscious focus, if you will—move away from the focal plane and explore that of which it can become aware within the peripheral field—let it roam around within the peripheral field. *In short, "visual focus" and "conscious focus" are, for the moment, parting company.* In this little experiment we experience an analogy to consciousness's ability to separate itself from its usual dimension of "focus," and, *while still focused, still aware*—start to access and peruse a different mindscape.

As I hold my forward gaze, there is a sense of

motion that is highly noticeable in the peripheral field. I notice, for instance, a small flock of birds (probably starlings), perhaps 150 feet from where I'm sitting, taking wing at about 30 degrees to the right of my visual point of focus. The motion of breeze-tweaked leaves is all over the visual field, and the dark trunks of trees are discernible throughout. Just the awareness that conscious attention/conscious focus can move and roam *anywhere* within the visual field without relying on changing the visual focal point brings into the realm of conscious perception the immensity of the entire visual field itself—taken all of-a-piece—a kind of "taking it all in" that eludes our awareness during our usual, consciously focused experience of vision along the focal plane. This experience of such a new way of *conscious* seeing can be a real eye-opener. Objects that are stationary are harder to make an object of conscious attention in the peripheral field, but as soon as there is motion *anywhere* within the extended visual field, the motion (and the objects in motion) come to life, and can stand out quite vividly—be surprisingly distinct and observable.

Indeed, you may notice that *it's possible that much in the extended peripheral field is still quite resolvable as objects, even though they be at some variance from the actual focal plane!*

I mentioned earlier the flock of starlings which were so accommodating as to take flight while I was consciously perusing my visual periphery in the course of writing this. Yet it turns out that this flock of starlings, some 30 degrees off axis from my visual focus, was not a smudge or a blur at all; the individual members of this flock were actually observable, as individuals, even when observed out on the periphery like this. This suggests that sharp images are being focused on the back of the eye-ball (retina), but because they are off-axis from the neurological systems responsible for the resolving and processing of visual images into objects (the kind of processing we associate with those images held within the visual focal plane) these peripheral images are not processed in a resolve-the-image kind of way, although at the level of lens, cornea, iris, retina and back of the eyeball, these "peripheral" images may be just as sharp and distinct, optically, as those which are taken up along the focal plane: that which we think of as "visual focus."

It may be that prior to having actually brought "conscious seeing" to bear on the peripheral field of vision, we simply assume that anything in the area outside the focal plane is blurry or hazy or "out of focus." How startling it is to realize that this is not necessarily so! It is, perhaps, only the blurriness of the conscious attention rendered to the greater periphery that accounts for the assumption that objects held within the periphery are "blurry" because they are "out of focus."

Indeed, at times there is not much, actually, that is blurred or smudged within it! How odd it is, then, first to discover that conscious attention can "separate" from visual focus—can move anywhere around the peripheral field, can make any area within the

The Visual Play of Consciousness

extended visual field the "object" of conscious focus without any change in *visual* focus—and how odd it is to discover that the extended visual field, as assayed by roving conscious attention, is not really a field of smudges or blurs at all, but has "things" in it at quite a high level of distinctness. And, further, how odd it is, having discovered that the periphery contains detailed "things," to have to make the distinction that although the sharpness of detail of "things" in the periphery is discernible, there is, as yet, some qualitative difference between highly articulated things that are not on the focal plane and those same highly articulated things once placed on the focal plane—and that *this* difference, whatever it is, does not really have to do with the clarity of objects at the level of optical detail. There is some *other* difference present between "peripheral objects" and objects held in the focal plane, and visual detail, per se, is not necessarily the determining factor in this difference!

Observing this over and over again, seeing the detail of objects in the peripheral field and contrasting the difference in cognition of these peripheral-field objects with cognitions of objects on the focal plane, can be quite a tease—with all of this comparing and contrasting occurring while the faculty of conscious attention, as a mode of cognition, is, unto itself, uniform throughout.

Moreover, further evidence delineates the possibility not only of peripheral objects' not being a "smudge," but even of their being, at times, *observable* with as *much* clarity and specificity—affording the same or similar levels of cognition (and therefore having been subjected to similar kinds of neurological processing) as those that we pointedly look at on the focal plane. (There may be parts of [our] consciousness—I could refer to them glibly as "unconscious parts," but what may be "unconscious" about them may not be *their* own, intrinsic experience of unconsciousness, but, rather, our lack of awareness of *them*—which are capable of observing, resolving and processing remarkable levels of detail and distinctness as exist within the peripheral visual field.) Evidence of this is anecdotal, but perhaps is enticing enough to encourage some experimentation in this area.

The first anecdotal evidence for this comes from prolonged experience with "keeping an eye on the tape"—in this instance the stock market ticker, initially (many years ago) as flickering across a wall in a brokerage office, and in more recent years parading at the bottom of the television screen on the networks FNN, CNN and then CNBC, during the hours of stock market activity. What I have repeatedly noticed is that when I have an interest in a company, and therefore have an interest in monitoring trading in the securities of that company, the three or four (or more) letter "symbol" which, as the abbreviation for the company's securities, designates a trade having occurred in the stock of the company, will be "noticed" by some very observant part of me, apparently capable of fine levels of resolution even though the symbol for the stock,

The Visual Play of Consciousness

when first noticed, is way out in the peripheral field. (My conscious gaze may often be directed elsewhere, not even looking at the video screen.) Some aspect of "me" is capable of recognizing and resolving these peripheral images—perhaps (since the focal plane is elsewhere) in a manner different from focal-plane resolution and visual processing—but no less effective! I have noticed (and noted) this experience hundreds of times, and it never fails to amaze me. All "I" am aware of is a sudden involuntary jerking of my head to bring my focal plane around to align with what has *already* been perceived and noted at a fine level of detail.

As a conscious experience, I then see the lettered symbol proceeding across the screen, and acknowledge it consciously, and acknowledge as well the "consciousness" that has powers of seeking, finding and resolving "out there on the periphery," the visual suburbs—and, moreover, has the power, immediately following its perception, to direct *my* conscious attention to what it has already seen: a specific ticker symbol in which I have explicit interest. Meanwhile, the thousands of (to me) irrelevant ticker symbols that parade by each trading day never jerk my head.

Two implications of this experience are: (1) there are means of observing and processing peripheral images that are finely attuned to, and responsive to, remarkable levels of detail and distinctiveness of these images, notwithstanding their being far removed from the focal plane, and (2) there is a part of our being which, unbeknownst to us, has access to this alternative way of seeking and processing peripheral images even though "I," in ego form, do not have this.

The other area of anecdotal relevance which has come to my attention over the years is in the clinical treatment of multiple-personality clients. I have witnessed any number of instances in which concurrent, simultaneous experiences of an utterly different quality and character have been subsequently reported by two or more alter personalities who, nominally, were conjointly "present" in the body (and therefore present to an external environment) at the same time, with each present and observing alter's being unaware that the other (or others) was (were) "present." Each present and observing alter reported a different experience occurring for him/herself, respectively, involving separate, yet concurrent, goings on within the overall visual field. In a typical (*not* atypical) report, one alter personality would be primarily "in the body"—having executive control over body movement, *including* visual focus—and subsequent alters would, unbeknownst to the first, be co-present as simultaneous, observing consciousnesses. However these additional alters would be observing simultaneous, off-axis—i.e., off focal plane—details and occurrences in contradistinction to the more-fully-in-the-body alter (who would be reporting only focal plane-aligned events). In the combined reports I have noted there does not appear to be any qualitative lessening of observational richness regarding events, details, and goings on noted as occurring in what we would consider the extended peripheral field of view versus those reported along the focal plane. This is highly suggestive of there existing, within us, alternative means through which peripheral images can be, and are, processed to remarkable degrees of fineness, *and* that there are other-than-the-customary-ego-based aspects of our own consciousness—our own being—alternative consciousnesses within us—which (who) do precisely that.

✧ ✧ ✧

Much of what has been already written in this little chapter addressing vision as one playground of consciousness has implicitly involved *gazing*, which can be thought of as the "holding of a 'soft' focus" on some point. Gazing is usually arrived at by establishing a "hard focus" on a point, and then, in a sense, de-tuning (disaligning!) slightly. Not that the point of focus changes. It doesn't. But relaxing from a hard focus to a soft focus—a gaze—seems to broaden out a sense of the periphery as an expansion of the focal plane, i.e., one becomes conscious of the periphery as a simultaneous experience along with, and inclusive of, the focal plane.

We, therefore, used "gazing" as a way to explore, initially, the breadth and scope of the visual field, and we used it to open our perception of how our conscious focus could move around anywhere within the visual field (could graze anywhere within the field of gaze!).

We also used gazing as we assessed the unsuspected distinctness of the delineations of motion, forms and objects in the peripheral field of vision as we duly made each of these a focus of conscious attention, even as we held our gaze-focus steady, elsewhere.

It is time to speak a bit more about the consciousness of gazing. Find a tree to sit up against and a near-field landscape that is quite uniform. This can be branches, or grass, or trees, or flowerbeds, or even a textured or patterned concrete playground or wall of bricks, or a pattern of shadows cast by leaves upon the ground. Pick a point of focus somewhere in the middle of the visual field—focusing perhaps on a single pebble, or a twig, or a flower or flower stalk, or an irregularity in a concrete pattern or mosaic of brickwork—something easy to stay focused on. After establishing your hard focus, "ease off" into soft focus—a gaze—while holding the same point of focus.

Now ... relax, hold still, blinking as infrequently as possible ... and await developments.

It is likely that, as you hold your soft focus, swirling geometric patterns will start to "impose" themselves upon whatever your field of view contains. As you continue to hold still, these patterns will become more strident, building in intensity. They will assert themselves in curious ways, sometimes appearing "constructed" of "motions" of things in the visual field, at other times consisting of the interplay of visual color, contrast and form throughout the visual field. At some point these geometric patterns—impositions—may become the dominant feature of what is happening within vision. Indeed, there may be a building to a spontaneous eruption of visual patterning, sometimes as "bands"—undulating parallel waves of energetic brightness—working across the visual field. Or they may appear as circular patterns that start as light-agitation—the shimmering of light—around the whole edge of the periphery, and then fluctuate in, concentrically, towards the center of focus (or they may sometimes commence around the focal plane and radiate, concentrically, outwards through the periphery). A complete eruption of these patterns of imposition may consist of ten to fifteen distinct emanations of the wave disturbances, one right after another, perhaps lasting, in toto, for a minute or more. The patterned nuance and detail which get "highlighted" during such an eruption is startling in its beauty and subtlety.

It seems that, within the held gaze, the neurology of visual processing, which appears at all times to be cued by the motion of objects, or by the constant changing of the focal point itself (which creates the illusion of objects' being in motion) gets defeated by a held focus, and, so to speak, doesn't know what to do with itself. A held focus, in very short order, gives the visual processing system nothing customary to process! As the neurological processing faculty (network) continues to "scan" for input to process, *it reveals itself*. No longer a seamless function to vision—to sight—to seeing—it reveals itself in all its pervasiveness, unmasked as to its prominence within our every experience of sight. What we are "seeing" at such times is our own neurology of seeing. What consciousness is seeing are the "tracks in the bubble chamber" made by the particles of itself. Indeed, we don't see our "eye," but we do see something of how our eye "sees"—of how we "see."

As we become accustomed to gazing, our conscious "focus" moves from visual focus, per se, *to encompass*, all of a piece, the entire visual field. The visual focal plane is not abandoned; it is now part and parcel of the larger conscious focus.

And as we become accustomed to this way of "seeing," something of great moment is apt to occur. It is almost as if, with a flip of the cat's cradle, the dimensionality of the entire visual field collapses. Near-field and far-field become amalgamated into one mosaiced pattern, and as this happens we suddenly, ourselves, become immersed in the field—surrounded, permeated, encompassed by, suffused with, *it*. And with this collapse of dimensionality we are absorbed into the field itself—not as observer—but as a consciousness indistinguishable from what is being observed. We are absorbed into a dimensional collapse even as, once absorbed, we become an immensity, an immense volume which we live and breathe—which lives us and breathes us—in every moment. We lose our locus—our coordinates as a separate being, as a separate entity—and pulse with creation. Yet our lucidity is vivid. Are we, within such moments, crossed over into alternate realities, or, perchance, alternate assemblages of a more encompassing reality? Is this point the most rudimentary form of cross-dimensional traveling? If so, what discoveries may await those explorers of consciousness who venture "across the gap" for ever more extended periods?[3]

---

3) In one beautiful irony, as I was immersed in a final edit of this chapter (January, 2010), my labors coincided with my going to see an optometrist in San Francisco to get my vision—and eyes—thoroughly checked. Technology continues to march! For the first time in many such appointments, images were taken of the back of my retinas. I was able to behold the magnificence of the morphology of the ocular seat of vision. What unspeakably beautiful images those mandalas are! Seeing the gorgeous asymmetry of the veins bundling in to the eyeball along the plane of the optic nerve—the actual physical basis of the "blind spot"—then spreading throughout, and held within, the fullest of the pastel-shaded, golden glow of a low-to-the-horizon rising full-moon, I was struck dumb at the beauty of it all. The thoughts ensuing quickly on the heels of witnessing these images were melded with the emotion of awe (a rare experience for me), that I, even in the most prosaic experience of myself as one unexceptional member of the human family, have such an exquisite embodiment as a carrier of vision—and of my consciousness, and my earthly identity. Witnessing a personal image of the timeless beauty of creation that carries us is a perspective-altering experience, now available to anyone.

Who's At Home In Your Body (When You're Not)?

The Consciousness of Familiarity/Unfamiliarity

Some time ago I noticed something about dreams. I noticed that we often traverse from a context, *within* a dream, in which the major particulars are felt to be known and utterly familiar to us—a context in which this sense of familiarity itself is one of the pronounced qualities of a dream—to one in which we are, once outside the dream, observing fleetingly receding details within a context that, as we reflect upon them in a wakeful (non-sleep) state, feel thoroughly unfamiliar and "other"—alien, even.

How is it that the familiarity we experience within dreams, which takes on such a ruddy hue in this altered state, feels so cut off and disconnected—unrelated to us in our "grounded" awake state?

We needn't even resort to the relationship we experience between dreamland and awake-land to ponder this contrast. Although the transition from dreaming (within sleep) to being awake (in our daily lives) lends us a rapidity of contrast within which we can see the fleeting, quirky and shifting quality of familiarity/unfamiliarity, within the extended course and flow of our "awake" lives we can also, most certainly, notice and reflect upon the ebb and flow of familiarity and unfamiliarity as these qualities play out in our relations with other people, places and circumstances.

While, within our wakeful lives, the shift in these experienced qualities is usually not as swift as that encountered in the transition from "asleep" to "awake," it is at least as impressive and distinct, once considered independent of the time dimension (rapidity of transition).

For instance, if we ponder the sense of familiarity/unfamiliarity that accompanies intimate relationships—*especially* those that have gone the distance in the direction of living out, and then outliving, their intimacy—we are left to reconnoiter changes in the perception of familiarity/unfamiliarity that are truly extreme.

At the outset of any such relationship, unfamiliarity is penetrated by a spark of interest—intrigue, attraction, coincidence, mutual discovery and the like—which lets in, for both parties, a shaft of shared curiosity. A dredging operation ensues in which each reclaims land from the sea of the mysteriosum of the other, and erects dikes to keep the ever waiting ocean of the infinite from inundating shared, reclaimed land. With each dredging operation additional psychical land is drained, broken to the plow, made arable to the planting and pruning hands (and intentions) of each partner. Shared space may be perceived quite differently by each one, but they both draw their perceptions from the same basic tract. A sense of familiarity — the known, the reliably recurring, the predictable — arises for each partner from this shared terrain, regardless of how differently each perceives it.

An amazing edifice of life-structure — of emotional constancy — comes to be emplaced thereupon. Personal identity becomes woven into, and derived from, the reliable texture, cultivation, crop and yield of this shared space. Once established, deepening familiarity arises within itself, assuming the mantle of a "given" — of a pre-existing emotional calibration of shared history and solidarity. In other words, anything or anyone that (who) makes it over the hurdle to having familiarity conferred upon it (him/her) becomes experienced as *always* having been familiar. How often has two lovers' initial experience of each other been expressed as that of feeling, "I've always known you, and you have always known me, and we open ourselves to each other so completely and seemingly without effort!"

So familiarity becomes our psyche's way of calibrating us to demystify and incorporate the foreign, or alien, so that we may experience it as part of who we are — and rock solid at that. Once familiarity is thereby conferred, it tends to be taken *as* granted, and events that might lead us to raise questions concerning the premise — now become uncritical acceptance — on which familiarity is founded (and that might raise issues regarding its possible transiency) tend to be resisted, disregarded and otherwise cast aside.[1]

If only life were polite enough to let things be as they stand at this point!

Unfamiliarity, as a feeling, is, in a way, our grounded state regarding that which we don't know. However, how many of us can grasp that *that* which comprises our range of the familiar—of familiarity—whether family, friends, colleagues, intimates and confidants, places, things, conditions, personal histories, stations in life, and so on—can recede back into the vast range of the unfamiliar to such an extent that we can be left, in hindsight, *incredulous* that a sense of prior familiarity *ever* existed between us and whatever?! It is one thing to experience the range of the unfamiliar as that which we feel we have never known; it is quite another to experience the shift between us and something once known and cherished—to watch qualities of unfamiliarity emerge in that which has been most intimately known and most-assumed to be stable for us in our lives—even to see, metaphorically, the ocean of untamed wildness break through our once rigid dikes, encircling the "familiar," and inundate,

---

[1] "Defiance" (a form of denial) has been defined as that quality which, in the person who has it, enables him or her to snap his or her fingers in the face of reality, and live on unperturbed. (Harry M. Tiebout, M.D. "The Act of Surrender in the Therapeutic Process." *Quarterly Journal of Studies on Alcohol*, 1953.) Available online at www.silkworth.net/tiebout/tiebout_papers.html. All of Tiebout's papers make for evocative reading. They are seminal treatises on psychological dynamics bearing particular relevance to addictive disorders.

The Consciousness of Familiarity/Unfamiliarity

re-arrange, and even reclaim our once-upon-a-time mutually arrived at, dredged, tilled, cultivated, harvested and shared habitat. And with the extinguishing of familiarity comes the biggest blow of all—the loss of the sense that there *ever was* a shared basis for intimacy, for knowing and being known, for trusting, for commonality and communitizing.

Once the shock of disillusionment wears off (if it ever does) following the retrenchment of the familiar back into the background of the unfamiliar, we are left to ponder the meaning of these qualities, and the illusion they pose regarding their apparent foundation and constancy.

Of course this *unfamiliar ⟶ familiar ⟶ once again unfamiliar* sequence can sometimes unfold in reverse, with assumed familiarity at the outset giving way to alienation/estrangement (the unfamiliar) only to be infused with familiarity once again further down the line. (When expressed this way, the sequence starts to take on a "chicken-or-the-egg?" quality.)

Perhaps the most impressive discovery about the consciousness of familiarity/unfamiliarity is that it is self-validating; it coronates itself—its validation of itself is intrinsic to the experience. This self-fulfilling validation suggests that these states of familiarity and unfamiliarity exist intrinsically—unto themselves. They, as a priori, color our world and are often taken as being synonymous with the objects (people, places, things, etc.) onto which they are cast or conferred. Critical acceptance (or rejection) be damned! The clue for this is, once again, to be taken from the dream experience in which the *sensation* of familiarity regarding dream images (objects), outlandish ones notwithstanding, is, while dreaming, often compelling and convincing, even though this sensation frequently arises in the absence of any historical, real-life referents for those images.

So where, once we start to dispel the vapors around familiarity/unfamiliarity, does this leave us? Is there any enduring attachment or familiarity between, say, two people that can be trusted to "go the distance" within a lifetime—that can actually prove-out as having been (and being) founded upon qualities of discernment intrinsic to each partner rather than as constituting an opportunistic, temporary way-station serving the self-absorbed vagaries of their underlying souls? Maybe—*but* it won't be by the mere presence of the feeling of familiarity alone that the solidity of such a knowing will be demonstrated. Indeed, regardless of the presence of the feeling of familiarity, it may be that this presence need always be lived out as if one remains a water-treader in the midst of a sea of unknowing, regardless of whether one feels draped in a bathing suit of felt familiarity or not.

So once again, if familiarity itself validates only its own quality of feeling, but can not conclusively validate anything underlying it, is there any other means to know if familiarity is solidly based?

Yes. The consciousness of familiarity/unfamiliarity may be more substantially validated by a study of what gets created and left in its wake. If it is illusory only — recreating, reinventing, and reconstellating itself on a whim (which it's capable of doing) — then there is no *development* or refinement of consciousness arising from it, and its yield in the outer world is random, hit-or-miss, spurious. There is no bounty, either in what consciousness appropriates from the experience of the familiar, nor is there anything akin to a legacy left in its wake. The flexations of consciousness reveal themselves as barren.

If, however, the attachments on which familiarity is conferred yield an intrapsychic bounty of some sort (as able to be assessed only by looking in the rear-view mirror), then the picture changes. To truly experience familiarity with another is to undergo the adventure of fathoming the universe comprising each person and, by inference, any "thing" knowable. A true knowing of an "other" then leads us to encounter and experience the vastness which all true knowing holds if it be true. And in knowing this depth with another, one discovers it within oneself as it is revealed to oneself by the other, and is revealed by oneself to the other. Familiarity then challenges us to move beyond what seems safe and predictable in another and to venture into greater depths in which, paradoxically, it is mystery, rather than what is already known, that serves to deepen familiarity. Perhaps the ultimate longevity of a sustained consciousness of familiarity has more to do with a mutual moving into mystery by both knower and known, rather than with trying to tether familiarity to the illusory safety of that which is already assumed to be thoroughly known, and an irreducible given. Familiarity, if it be true, will not turn tail and bolt in encountering the unknown. It will once again strive to drain a new marsh.

Finally, through the mysteriosum of a thoroughly (though never completely) known "other," whether person, place, thing, and so on, durable relations of familiarity are discovered to exist with everyone, and with all things, everywhere and always.

Goose Bumps, Shivers & Body Slams: Embodying Consciousness's Exaltations

Many people experience goose bumps, shivers and "body slams." At a purely physiological level they may depict conditions directly pertaining to, and arising within, the body itself, as in, respectively, cold, fear and the rush of adrenaline.

But consciousness, of which the body itself is an extension, may often be a non-body source of these physiological manifestations. The experience of goosebumps, or of shivers running up and down one's spine may be in reality a bodily manifestation of consciousness's *own* experience of reverence, of awe, of beauty, of conscious connection with the Divine—and, as well, of being happy and *knowing* it!

"Body slams," or sudden, intense rushes of energy—of (often) tingling sensation—throughout the body, including the extremities, may, similarly, mirror sudden psychological insights or spiritual awakening.

Sometimes such "opening" of the body occurs in the apparent absence of any accompanying experience of a particular emotion or thought (or of cold or fear). Such openings, seemingly spontaneous, can serve, so to speak, to "open the door" of conscious perception into the realm of immediate and direct correspondence with the transcendent.

When one is becoming aware of the onset of such embodied responses, it is possible to learn to reside within them—even, through a combination of simultaneous observing and relaxing, to submerge one's being into them, and thereby extend one's experience of them in both depth and duration. In short, one can learn to bodysurf them. From such a sensing point, one's own bodily boundaries are suddenly as if transparent and permeable, and ranges of energy are felt to course through the body, radiating out from it even as the body itself extends its own capacities as an energy receptor. This simultaneous linking up of energy flow throughout the body, energy transmission arising from within the body, and energy reception by the open, receptive body, with the emotional sensitivities of awe or reverence can be akin to a lasing—a correlation of energies at coordinated levels of mind, body, spirit and heart, in which a coherent, encompassing, panoramic enmeshment within the Divine flux transpires.

Of course, the question arises: Just why should there be—how is it that there happens to be in the lives of so many—this correlation between conscious experiences of reverie, beauty or awe and, at the level of the body, goose bumps, tingles and surges? After all, from a purely evolutionary point of view there is no obvious survival advantage conferred by this coupling!

Perhaps the most direct way to address this point is to hypothesize that no experience of embodied consciousness is "complete" as an experience unless

Goose Bumps, Shivers & Body Slams

the very fact of being embodied is, itself, orchestrated along with any and all other perceptions or cognitions. Just as the experience of the emotions fear and terror are primarily "body"—and as visceral and wrenching as any retching born as a biochemical consequence of food poisoning—so, too, the bodily concomitants of exalted states of consciousness are also necessary parts of the complete orchestration of exaltation.

What is perhaps odd is that the *range* of bodily expression is essentially similar regardless of whether the states of consciousness from which they ensue are primarily exalted states or dismal ones.

Within the body there are numerous analogues for this: Tears of sorrow and tears of joy are still salt tears, and issue from the same glands and pour through the same ducts. The convulsions of hysterical laughter and the convulsions of heart-rending sobbing are still convulsive, deploying the same musculature and even the same rhythm (and, maybe, even drawing on the same energy of unconscious-based emotion). There are also the "tears for no apparent (felt) reason"—autonomous tears (not to mention the experience of crying out of one eye only)—and the "case of giggles" in which one is seized by a deliciously impish complex, usually in a situation where decorum is de rigueur and, entirely at odds with one's conscious intention, reduced to rubble through ill-stifled peals of hysterics ("giggle fits," we used to call them).

Yet the orchestration makes all the difference, for the tears within a meaning of sorrow are experienced as very different tears than those ushering in a feeling of joy, notwithstanding the moisture and the salt, and what is truly comical shapes an experience of convulsive, tearful laughter in ways far different than the convulsive sobbing of tragic loss or grieving, notwithstanding the involuntary explosiveness of both.

The goosebumps, surges and slams of embodied consciousness, then, in addition to serving the "grounded" emotions of local, everyday life, can also serve to ground consciousness's own exaltations and, in so doing, lend depth and a kinesthetically felt dimension to what otherwise would be cerebral reckonings only. As mentioned, they also, arising spontaneously, sometimes trumpet the opening of epiphany, and the mere attending to these phenomena and learning to swim and surf with them can loose the fetters of mundane, body-encased consciousness so that it can start to be transported—to soar and know itself as being breathed by the Infinite.

Another distinction worth making between the goose bumps, surges and slams of bodily origin only—the chills, fears and adrenaline of survival-based instinct and awareness—and those accompanying exaltation-consciousness, is that in fear-based reactions the body is generally alert in a way that is very tense and mobilized. In, experientially, crossing the barrier into a cognizance of exalted consciousness, however, one becomes aware that the goose bumps, surges and body slams, while no less an alert awareness, are altogether of a different tenor: The body is alert not in a tense way, but in a loose way. In place of a mobilized rigidity is a flow—an exchange—a breathing. The body's boundaries are not demarcated by isometric tension; they expand and contract with the "energy's" breathing of the body itself. Indeed, the boundaries cease being definite; they "take in," they "give out"; within one's mind's eye they may reach forth to the heavens and descend into the very depths of the earth, and, elastic as they are, they draw of it all into themselves, into the body-as-womb, ebbing and flowing between heaven and earth—between male and female.

When an opening occurs it may nearly coincide with a just-preceding thought, or upon hearing a certain piece of music or absorbing lines of poetry, or seeing a landscape or a sunset or a sunrise or a work of art, or occur as an epiphany of becoming lucid within a dream while (technically) "asleep." In such moments we can either make the connection between the opening and the apparent stimulus, or we can ride the opening itself, *for its own sake*, regardless of precipitating events, discovering, as we nurture ourselves along within it, where it takes us.

So when they: the goose bumps, surges and slams of our neurology, show up, it may well be worth minding them—making attending to them the instant priority of the moment. They respond to being so honored by extending their stay, and by making their visits more frequent. They, far from being a reward for an ascetic disregard of, and escape from, the body's own sensorium, are, rather, an enrichment arising from integrating and assimilating — even rejoicing in — that very sensorium, the reality of having a body in which to have and hold life in a four-dimensional space-time existence. They celebrate, and validate, the grounded body state which, in the overall scheme of things, is our intentional abode within this lifetime we know.

And yet, in their own way, our goose bumps, energy surges and body-slams reveal to us that life in a body is not inconsistent with spiritual connection — that exalted consciousness itself can make itself felt — and even become at home — in the body itself. Indeed, it may just be that conscious exaltations, through being in-corporated — i.e., through being a part of bodily expression — may, within the extended soul and psyche, *only* be assimilable in this fashion. Indeed, this may be one of the functions that bodily existence serves.

Of course, my own speculations on such matters may well be very far off the mark; however, the fact that these occurrences can even lead to quite serious musings about their meaning, and the role of bodily existence in hosting them concretely, suggests that, *whatever* the meaning hidden within them, they are not trivial phenomena. Their richness may, indeed, even be that they spur the meaning-making function within us, stretching us conceptually and philosophically as they do so.

If the goose bumps, energy surges and body slams are not your thing — are alien to you — then perhaps your body (and neurology) have other pathways for manifesting the physicality of conscious exaltation. A warm feeling in the tummy, or (as previously mentioned) the unaccountable "tears of joy" would be just two manifestations of possibly a very wide range of expression.

Perhaps the underlying question, to which each of us can attend, is: "*How* am I moved?" If something moves me, what is the *embodied* portion of this feeling or emotion? Of course, the question, "*What* moves me?" is also important, for that which moves me—whatever it/they may be—sets the context for the body's response. However, attention paid to "How does being moved manifest in the body?" will start to make conscious the physical pathway itself, regardless of any specific outer-world situation that may, within any given moment, be evoking the physical response. Once we know the pathway of response, we know the pathway through which we may be—and may be being—"reached."

Eventually, we may, just possibly, find the exaltation of consciousness, with its awe, beauty and reverence, available to us as intrinsic to the pathway itself, and no longer experienced as depending solely upon the presence of *any* precipitating events to trigger it. Such a consciousness of exaltation then leads to ongoing experiences of awe, beauty, reverence and bliss as part and parcel of all our experiences—both inner and outer—regardless of however sublime or mundane apparent precipitating events might otherwise appear, even while, in its essence, our embodied participation in exaltation is revealed, and known, as existing independent of all of them.

Just maybe such experiences are the essence of sheer "presence."

The Consciousness of Newness

The consciousness of newness is the scope of consciousness encompassing both the possession of some cherished, unblemished, perfect thing—something that is especially prized just because it is new and unblemished (rather than merely valued for its utility)—*and the threshold that consciousness crosses in which the cherished thing comes down off the display pedestal and takes up its rightful place as another functional life-accessory.*

Buying, or receiving, a new thing provides us a study in perfection. To take delivery of a new car, or a new appliance, or some new toy is to have—as long as the car remains freshly buffed and on the dealer's lot (unexposed to actual driving), the appliance remains in the carton, and the new toy stays untouched and untested—an actual experience of possessing the perfect.

How consciousness relishes this! It's as if something has come down to us, intact, from the Platonic world of ideas, of perfect forms—so pristine, so unmarked, so utterly chaste and unspoiled.

Consciousness's first response to being so gifted is to protect the newness, the perfection, by minimal use — or even none at all (the true collector!) — by loving, tender nurturance (rituals of exacting maintenance and beautification), by preserving the pristineness. Perfection, in this sense, seems "on loan" to us, and we are its stewards.

Of course, such a betrothal to perfection is, truly, Platonic in more ways than one, for, in the perfect preservation of perfection, perfection never meets (can never cross paths with) the utility of practical usage — the "where the rubber meets the road" (to borrow from an old auto tire advertisement) of actual deployment, of being "placed in service." Usage always entails wear and tear, depreciation, aging and maintenance, and the maintenance, after a point, is no longer to preserve the qualities of a museum specimen, but rather to maintain road-worthiness, utility, and serviceability.

Notwithstanding its initial sense of cherishing, the consciousness of newness gives way, unavoidably, from protecting the pristine, to embracing, without much thought or rapture, practicality.

Is it the first (or the fifth or the eighteenth) dent in a fender or scratch on a virginal paint job that pulls consciousness across this divide? Is it that first (or the ninth or the thirty-first) spill or stain on the upholstery that ferries consciousness on over? Can it happen all-at-once, as in the sudden and extensive despoiling of a new car's body and windshield by a hail of pebbles and gravel as flung up from some unkempt, jouncing truck sprinting along a highway—a moment in which "newness" is massively, irretrievably compromised?[1]....Or is it, perhaps, a more gradual process of acclimatization in which consciousness wearies of the sharp focus of unalloyed attention and attentiveness required to keep the perfect specimen elevated and protected? Is it, maybe, a distractedness in which attention gives up its hold on the perfect just long enough to tend to some other momentary imperative, during which some regularly scheduled routine maintenance—of maintaining beautification (beatification?)—gets overlooked, and a trend towards tolerated "wear" sets in? Is it that moment when consciousness knowingly accepts "wear" without instantly attempting to—at least cosmetically—reverse it or eliminate its outer signs? (And could a similar trend be noted regarding, for instance, the releasing of our fancied hold on our own relative youthful perfections of body—and our fervent attempts to freeze them via face-lifts, tummy tucks, boob-jobs, botox, liposuction, diets and compulsive fitness regimens—the transcending of

---

[1] This happenstance actually befell me in the very course of writing this essay (July, 2000). I was heading west on Route 2 by the Route 495 overpass (about 25 miles west of Boston, MA). I was following a large dump truck, which was really barrel-assing along the highway. I was the next vehicle behind the truck, though not that close to it. Encountering a construction zone, the behemoth started jouncing wildly, and sheets upon sheets of gravel were ejected out over the top of the container, liberally strafing my poor little new car with several fusillades of projectiles (ejectiles?). Instant despoiling.

our own vanity as to our appearance, and the tacit acceptance of the scourges of "wear and tear," along with the unavoidable adventures (and misadventures) in decrepitude that advancing age holds for us?)

However, or whatever, this transition of consciousness is (whether sudden or cumulative), and regardless of whatever specific events precipitate it, unless one is in the museum business or the collectibles business to a degree bordering on the obsessional, *it always happens*. The "dings" outweigh the "blings," becoming a part of what was once perfect. Utility becomes, de facto, more important than unblemished, even chiseled, beauty.

Indeed, perhaps the perfect needs to take on blemishes so that it may descend to us, meeting us where we live in our world of wear, of aging, of breakage, of application, of refurbishment, of functional add-ons, accelerator boards and modifications, of patch-ups, mends and up-grades.

In making this descent, the "new" lets its major feature—perfection—become tempered and enlarged by *character*. From the standpoint of character, perfection is more a *process of perfecting* rather than a photo-op of final arrival—of some "mission accomplished," or a freeze-framed moment at the end of an assembly line surrounded by foam peanuts, form-fitting Styrofoam, heavy-gauge cardboard and packing tape. For character, the process of perfecting has everything to do with a kind of refining that comes *only* from being used—and even used up! *That* kind of perfecting sacrifices the still frames of isolated perfect moments

The Consciousness of Newness

and features, and submits to the bumping and grinding of life, the wear and tear and burnishings of triumphs and failures—the workings and weatherings of applied existence—of living.

This "perfecting" brand of perfection takes satisfaction in a good mend, an innovative repair, a "good as new"—i.e.: serviceable—approach to functionality. One comes to breathe with one's possessions, then, for they, no longer new, come along with us on our journeys through life. We come to relate to them as older and seasoned, as sturdy, as "tried and true"—and the more venerable for all that. That old, steerable, Flexible Flyer sled, tucked away for most of the year in some cobwebbed corner of the basement—a sled with *real* steel runners and belly-bumping platform (and steering handles) of aging oak interlaced with the iron, captures for us, not the pristineness of Platonic forms as flashed to us (once upon a time) through a department store display window or a catalogue's "popping" glossy image, but the stuff of our own climbs and descents through many winters. Within those many nicks and gashes on the wood and dents in the frame and creases in the runners is inscribed our life of swooping experience—our own encounters of rough and tumble, of side-to-side buffetings, of trudges up and slides on down. The sled's character is now inscribed—a grooved record of our own.

So to what, finally, does the consciousness of newness give way? We've traced its course, after a fashion, from protector of the pristine to deployer of the utilitarian—from museum specimen curator to maintainer of the serviceable, from valuing a static notion of perfect beauty, "features" and perfection to yielding to the acquisition of character through hoeing down with the grind and grist of day in, day out, usage, wear, tear and repair in a process of "perfecting."

The consciousness of newness gives way, then, to what we might call the consciousness of passage, in which perfection is still preserved (after a fashion) as the framed snapshots of a thing—static, soulless—frozen in time, and "passage" is lived as the motion and flow—the progression—of all things from "OEM's" (Original Equipment Manufactures) to "OOS" (Out of Service). The consciousness of newness, as it softens, comes to realize that to spare no quarter in preserving the original perfection of a thing is to be possessed by the thing itself, tantamount, in extreme cases, to a forfeiture of an evolving life of personhood and the perfecting of character.

Such a constricted life does not—indeed, cannot—age well, for in refusing to age—refusing to become soiled—it becomes, as time rushes by around it, a ghoulish anomaly in which its captured and imprisoned perfection holds only sterility. There is no "juice"—no descendable beauty—that comes down and meets us where we are, where the world actually lives and works, and finds its destiny.

With the advent of the consciousness of passage, a more mature sensibility recognizes, and responds to, an increasing beauty, of an altogether different sort, in the wear and the tear and the rough edges—and those occasional pearls of grace in which we take into *ourselves* the grit, and fashion our own character around it, layer-by-layer, line-by-line, wrinkle-by-wrinkle. Bearing with its imperfections, even suffering unrelentingly at the strength and insistence of the tethers of time ever yanking us *away* from any static perfection we may ever momentarily realize, a fullness, and maybe even a sense of completeness, arise for us as we increasingly relent, and let the dusty old world meet us only as dust, abrading and sculpting us as it does so.

Our sweet sadness at the passing of perfect features into the grounded beauty of weathered weariness—of the perfecting of character—establishes our place in the world, in which the pretense of who we once thought we were *supposed* to be, either as "newly minted" or "having it made," is erased by a comfort we find in being, ourselves, serviceable and resilient—at ease within our own skins (whether dry, moist, scaly, wrinkled, mole-ridden, age-spotted, freckled, talcum-soft or alabaster-smooth—warts and all). Our descent, once digested, brings us more into the world as self-evident embodiments of substantial consciousness—as who we are *meant* to be. Whether considered to be "educated" and well mannered (as might befit the perfect gentleman or lady) or not, we each, in our own manner, become repositories of interesting knowledge and *individualizing* features, ever added to by the consciousness of passage.

Unlike the consciousness of perfection, which must

resist the passage of time and what time represents, the fully developed consciousness of newness, as it comes to include "passage"—life in the world—is fed by it. Under such a sway, the march of time loses its bite and venom. There is only ripening of soul, which snacks on time at its leisure.

The Consciousness of Grace

*If Justice is getting what you deserve, and
Mercy is not getting what you deserve, then
Grace is getting what you don't deserve.*
  —anonymous

Grace is usually thought of as an unmerited gift—as something that comes to one, perhaps as a kind of intercession, or a materialization of unanticipated support or blessing.

Most people don't view the fashioning of their lives as a course through which they may become as channels—conduits for the carrying of a kind of grace that may be directed towards another, and even all others.

The awareness, as a living presence, that our lives hold meaning for us to just about the extent that they can provide avenues through which the grace of well-being and experienced safe passage can reach others—and that such a function most fully exemplifies the realization of our *own* capacity for wholeness and well-being and completeness—*is* the consciousness of grace.

One doesn't come by this consciousness easily, for what each of us has to offer in a grace-conveying role is not our "goodness," as narrowly defined. What each of us has to contribute through our acts of grace is our own *completeness* as a conscious, redeemed being.

Neither is this completeness come by "on the cheap." It includes everything there is about us: our hopes and dreams, our personal failures and flaws, our capacities (regardless of intention) to wound as well as heal, our pettinesses as well as our triumphs of character, our spiritual impoverishment and mean-spiritedness as well as our raptures, elevations and exaltations. One has to "get real" before one can "get good."

How many of us can actually embrace a concept of wholeness, completeness and grace that can include such a conscious, even intimate, knowing of the worst that is within us? How many of us can actually embrace a concept of wholeness which is inclusive of all that we are and everything we have ever thought or done, rather than something that stems from some lopsided realization of fancied virtue?

And how many of us can come to *consciously* experience ourselves as useful — as fulfilled in our life's calling — in being fashioned as Grace's instrument in a way that is both so extensive and so inclusive?

The immensity of this consciousness is awe itself. It involves the deepest inner warmth and inner knowing of the ultimate rightness of all that has happened and befallen us, no matter whether we have been inundated and decimated — and regardless whether that has come to us unbidden, from without or

The Consciousness of Grace

whether we have been slaughtered by our own hand. It involves the sure conviction that full personhood is an inalienable accomplishment which neither time nor any circumstance can ever wither. It is the quietness of a fullness that needn't run, nor shrink, from anything. It is a living, breathing current of redemption-achieved that is now ever present—ever at the ready to flow beyond the boundaries of personal selfhood to those who are receptive and in need. Such quiet, full assurance of self has the power, through its sheer presence, to awaken others. Spiritual bloodline—the more anonymous the better—issues from this.

The effects that radiate from an evolved spirit—from the consciousness of Grace—are profound even should that spirit choose to remain in the background or out of sight.

The consciousness of Grace takes its shots in every encounter—both with those known and those unknown. Such a state seems the common denominator of spiritual odyssey in all things and places and at all times. It hunts for kindred resonance everywhere, sensing the responsive presence regardless of where it arises, and quickening as it awakens to reunion with kin.

In the certitude of its quietude and intention it simply is, and radiance is that energy that characterizes it.

The sense of having been touched by a divine hand—first when in need, and then subsequently as a vehicle through which others in need can be reached—is a truly beautiful context in which to experience life, regardless of whether this flow is encountered only occasionally, or whether it becomes a more continuous, companionable presence. This experience of being both the recipient and the conduit of such lightness of spirit has a leavening effect on everything around us and, equally as important, on the way we come to assess what we are about and wherein lies our true destiny.

The consciousness of Grace punctuates our lives with an affirmation that breaks us beyond the co-ordinates that normally demarcate our habitually narrow day in, day out experience of ourselves. It speaks of the realities of mercy and forgiveness—that consciousness which holds these kinds of assessments is truly operative in the Higher realms. Our daring and our courage to accept the experience of Grace as the Universe's response to *us* in the form of its own mercy and forgiveness is the most moving affirmation available to us that we are fully known and cherished—and belong in the Universe's scheme of things. Our own courage to acknowledge and accept Grace, despite whoever we think we are and whatever we feel we have done, is our own contribution to this dynamic of redemption.

It is the full inclusion of all that we have been—of all that we *are*—into this acknowledgment of Grace that so redeems us, and it is the totality of our redemption, inclusive of all that we take ourselves to be, that makes our presence—always in furtherance of good purpose—so potentially fecund and powerful in the lives of others.

Who's At Home In Your Body (When You're Not)?

The Discontinuities of Consciousness

A "startle" is a discontinuity in the thread of consciousness.

It is one thing to be startled by a loud noise, as in the backfiring of a truck, or as brought on by someone stealthily coming up behind you and making his presence known to you by suddenly clasping you, blindside, by the shoulders (or worse). In such incidents, one recovers from a spike-overload of this sort with an experience of "surprise!" at least felt and, depending on the nature of the surprise, sometimes exclaimed. So "surprise" is the suspension of consciousness through a disruption, followed by consciousness's own near-immediate reassembling of being present.

There are the "startles" of acute, transient sensory overload, as in a firecracker going off nearby or the sudden sound of the air horn on an eighteen-wheeler. There are also the startles of unanticipated events of all sorts: extremely good or bad news, for instance, or sudden witnessings of beautiful events—or works of art—or the "shock" value of poverty, cruelty and guerrilla art.

Aside from these fairly straightforward (though, to have "startle" value, always unanticipated) events from our macro-world, most of us (I'm guessing) would relegate startle experiences to the realm of that which transpires most often in the lives of infants and young toddlers. Indeed, the "startle response" is one of the most noted of early life behaviors.

Perhaps what may arise as being truly disconcerting is the awareness that our adult lives are also full of "startle" experiences—indeed, far, far more of them occurring far more often than we might suspect—*until* we become aware of them. (And our becoming aware of them doesn't stop them, either; it only makes them an object of study). This is no mere awareness that there are more trucks backfiring out there in the outer world than we previously realized. Rather, the discontinuities of consciousness arise from *within* us, and at times they are so bold and glaring that a truck could be driven right through them (with diesel engine's air horn blaring) and we would be none the wiser.

A conceit we maintain about our adult consciousness is that its thread of awareness is unbroken. However, in fact, our consciousness reassembles so quickly (usually) on the far side of a disruption that we, carried along within our consciousness, are often not even aware that a discrepancy in temporal continuity of attention has occurred.

Awareness of such an event is possible, however, if one wants to develop it.

Perhaps the range of phenomena in which such discontinuities arise both suddenly and rather continuously is in the area of the body's own "twitches," a product of the nervous system's spontaneous and sporadic firing. This is always going on, but is not generally noticeable unless one is lying down and approaching the edge of sleep. At such times, it is possible to be aware of these twitches—not merely as a spontaneous moment (a movement apparently arising within a leg or arm)—*but as an actual suspension of consciousness itself.* This is not merely a startle response in reaction to a sensory overload (as in a loud noise) but is, rather, *a seemingly simultaneous disruption of consciousness which happens to coincide with a twitch or momentary tremor in the body, rather than just following upon it.* The shutter-speed suspension and reassembling of consciousness is a *concurrent* part of the overall event itself, rather than a response to an overload.

One can never anticipate such an event in the sense of being able to "count down" to it. One always becomes aware that there has been a twitch that has extended, and included, a momentary disruption of consciousness only after the fact. And yet, with practice it seems that the interval between twitch/disruption of consciousness and awareness that there has just been a twitch/disruption of consciousness becomes, apparently, shorter and shorter to the point at which the awareness becomes virtually immediate to the experience.

It is all rather uncanny, really. Lying down and feeling utterly at rest, with consciousness musing wherever it will as a flowing, undulating ribbon of smoothness, out of nowhere it—the sequence—comes: twitch/discontinuity of consciousness/millisecond scramble of reorientation (the two occurrences happen *so* close together)—awareness that a discontinuity of consciousness has just occurred arising only as an artifact of the reassembling and reorientation—and then, finally, the "memory" of the twitch that was a simultaneity with consciousness's spike of dismemberment. The whole notion of "re-membering" takes on literal significance in this typical experience.

Again, it is not the strength of the twitch that is, in and of itself, disruptive to conscious orientation. The actual twitch itself is *subtle*, even, at times, hardly noticeable. It is "twitch" as a conscious *marker* designating one part of a simultaneous occurrence, the hallmark of which is a discontinuity in the thread of sustained consciousness, that is the point.

It continues to be humbling to encounter the fragility of our own continuity of consciousness as one of the pervasive features of life in the body. These discontinuities are all around, through and about us. Our everyday consciousness, moment by moment, is shot through with them. The sense that our consciousness is relatively seamless in attending to whatever it will in the outer world is consciousness's own delusion about itself, as it, unbeknownst to us (and maybe itself) partitions off, encapsulates and stores in isolation the discontinuities that continually plague it.

It is also humbling to start to consider the larger picture. How consistently are any of us really "here"—with present attention—even while utterly convinced that we are?

Where are "we," during such intervals of scramble—when our mind-creeks are, for the moment, neurologically dynamited? "We" reassemble, it's true, but that only resolves the moment even as it underscores how amazingly "not here" we have just been.

Dream Consciousness

To open ourselves to dreams as one source, and kind, of input, is to enlarge the scope of who we are. There is no avenue that brings us closer to a felt centrality that is "not-I"—not ego-based—and yet to which we, in ego-land, stand in intimate and, less the effort to know it, subordinate relations.

That which dreams convey—the consciousness which they hold and that they are—can provide us, sometimes when we are in direst need, both the foundation for comprehension and the emotional resolve to persevere, to go on. That dreams, at such crucial times, carry within them this foundation-making power in the absence of any outer-world support or affirmation speaks to their singular significance.

They are sourced within that part of us (which exists in each one of us) that resides outside of space and time. They can easily draw on the spatial and temporal in the weaving of their own fabric for a given night's magic carpet-ride, however the scope and kinds of condensations routinely accomplished in our dreams speak of a locus of assessment within them that is not limited by the local coordinates of embodied personhood that demarcate and circumscribe us within our wakeful lives.

The magic, or enlargement, which accretes to us through the study and incorporation of dreams into our "awake" lives stems less from a clear understanding of dream content (although inscrutability may occasionally give way to pristine clarity) and more from the very fact of our acknowledging their existence, and our willingness to let ourselves be approached and engaged *by* them.

Prior to the conscious decision to be open to them, we stand as solitary as a period on a page. As the "dot," we are the "that's it," the "end of statement," the assertion of how "I" see it, in conscious relation with nothing more than the this-es and thats of emotion, spurious thought and conscious memory—our self-styled narratives—nothing deeper. With the decision to change the period to a question mark, followed by an ellipsis and a colon, we instantly, *just through this shift in attitude alone*, find ourselves on a continuum of self ←——→ other. We anchor down one end of it, and begin to stand in conscious relation with the other end—the "dream" end (as well as with all points in between).

At the outset, even without understanding much of dream language—even when it all seems like a mélange of textural gibberishes—we nevertheless start to develop the sense of being in active engagement with another culture. We aren't the only kids on the block, and we begin to comprehend that we never have been.

Dream Consciousness

And then, perhaps drawing heavily on our imagination — calling upon it to risk fanciful associations and unprovable speculations — this dream culture starts to unbundle, decipher and explicate itself before our amazed, half-awake eyes, and we sense the dream's own awareness that it has an audience, and that the dream (our dreams) are starting to play to that audience — us!

As dreams start to play to us, it seems that they, too, are looking for a point of contact, a point through which apprehension can be inaugurated, comprehension bridged, and mutual beachheads of encampment and correspondence established.

Perhaps one of the more startling realizations to arise through an open and honest engagement with our dreams is that we, in ego-land, do not live for ourselves alone. Our own limited awareness is a parcel of a larger, more encompassing consciousness which works to its own ends, regardless of our consent. However, *with* our "consent" — that is, acknowledgment — this more encompassing consciousness is more willing to "take us into account," to factor our awareness of it, and to a certain extent, our own conscious designs and priorities, into its equations. It even, on occasion, will come halfway to meet us, and it likes having its existence and its viewpoints acknowledged and "taken into account" by us.

Furthermore, dream consciousness, despite the multidimensional panorama from which it draws, operates at something of a disadvantage as it comes forward to meet and engage us, no matter how willing or open we may feel we are to encounter it. In order to reach us—to establish the bridge of comprehension—it is obliged to fashion, or tailor, that which it would reveal to us (or cajole us with) into representations and forms that stand some chance of gaining recognition by us in our embodied, culturally-conditioned four-dimensional space-time form. This is not an easy task for dream consciousness. It's a bit like attempting to render Victoria Falls into a form that can only flow through the eye of a needle—and yet, even so condensed and compressed as it re-emerges, a diminutive drop at a time, still be recognizable as Victoria Falls! What a handicap! However, our continued openness to our dream consciousness's attempts, however constrained they may be, to alter its renderings to us into forms that can be assimilated by our own ego-consciousness has the effect of *encouraging* dream consciousness towards greater refinements of its task, and dream consciousness can be highly creative and ingenious in rising to the task.

Our diligence in encountering and acclimating ourselves to the culture of dream consciousness helps it to bridge cultures. Our growing respect for the productions of dream consciousness elicits its respect—a kind of appreciation that we would even exert ourselves to solicit and appropriate its perspectives and, perhaps, even its counsel.

And as we work out our dialogue with dream consciousness, we *do* appropriate a portion of this consciousness. And as we appropriate a growing portion of this consciousness into our wakeful lives, it starts to become a working asset for us, day in and day out. The enlargement of personal consciousness resulting from our opening to dream consciousness grounds us in a larger experience of our being, one in which intuition and creative problem solving start to become companionable aspects of our daily lives. It may not even be overstating things to assert that with the incorporation of dream consciousness, we may come to experience our waking, daytime lives as if we are serving a stint at some outpost. Within this outpost there is, indeed, life: the society in which we find ourselves, our apparent station-in-life—the contexts in which we exist as we experience this wakeful reality. At night, however, we get to travel back into proximity to our soul center—the inner spiritual metropolis from which we develop certain perspectives, attitudes, and tasks which, in the aggregate, inform our life-at-the-outpost.

A shifting of the sense of our centrality as issuing more from the spiritual metropolis starts to set in. We, on our daily rounds, are just as much "in" the world, but not as much "of" the world.

And eventually, bit by bit, we experience a more unified consciousness that can straddle or move through either domain of consciousness in relative comfort—never beyond the potential to be shocked or prodded from within dream consciousness any more than we are ever completely insulated from shocks or upsets arising in our wakeful encounters with the external world. However, we are increasingly able to sample the delights and sublime intimations that a mature, more balanced consciousness yields to us, and these also carry over to, and color, our experiences in both the outer and inner worlds.

The evolution of the dialogue between who we are as personal, embodied, ego-beings and who we are at our fundaments (*inclusive* of ego-being, not exclusive of it) is open-ended. The richness and depth, the breadth and height of this relationship knows only the limits set upon it by comprehension—and this capacity is ever increasing.

As the dream dialogue grows, we no longer feel so crucially dependent upon any one feature of our external reality. People, places, things, situations, circumstances, environments, institutions, stations-in-life—all come and go as they will. With the dialogue born of dream consciousness and our willingness to engage it, we ascend to a more easeful way of riding life's currents, regardless of what may, or may not, be zephyring in or wafting through our life at any given time.

Counsel, humor, warning, rapture, assurance, solidarity, courage, even faith—all these qualities and attributes may be coronated and emboldened by a knowing participation in the consciousness of our dreams.

And yes (as alluded to earlier), once in a very great while, sometimes while we are in the midst of a crisis

Dream Consciousness

of some sort (but not even necessarily precipitated by such), a **BIG** dream comes along, and explicates to us—in ways that are lucid, direct, unambiguous, startling, multidimensional and *beyond* amazing—the precise nature and composition of our circumstance or predicament, within a combined, condensed context of past, present and future, as brought into absolute relief from numerous vantage points at once.

These are the dreams on which one can stake one's life (and may find it imperative to do so). Following the intimations of such a dream has, in my experience, *never* been a mistake.

From time to time it's natural to wonder: Am I the one who dreams these dreams, or am "I" merely a dream being generated and experienced by my own dream consciousness?

On a closing note, having been a close student of my, and others', dreaming lives/consciousness for over a quarter of a century, I have to confess to feeling a bit sheepish that virtually everything I have observed, learned and experienced regarding relating to dream consciousness can be condensed into so few pages.

Indeed, there are wonderful, compelling, learned and scholarly works on the nature of dreams available in any library, and over the years I have read, and been enriched by, a number of them. It may seem almost paltry, by comparison, that I actually have so little to write on the subject, given this background. And yet, notwithstanding a certain embarrassment, the brevity of this little chapter does seem to contain all that I know that can be safely generalized to all of you who would be (and will be) more active explorers of your dream consciousness.

To this end, may your respective, highly individual journeys into dream consciousness be rich, and come to sustain you. I am sure they will.

Obsession and Possession Consciousness

Obsession consciousness operates at the far end of the scale from enlightenment. If there is, within the notion of enlightenment, a sense of opening to a grand or greater vision, if there is a sense of consciousness's attaining to a panoramic experience in which a large swath of reality, in whatever dimension, can be taken in, and if, even, there is a sense of finding an opening to something universal through the fresh apperception of the commonplace, then the consciousness of obsession stands in stark contrast to all this.

For obsession consciousness carries within it a set of convincing delusions—the delusion that one's consciousness is expanding, rather than contracting or atrophying, and that *that* diminutive portion of reality which, at any given moment, constitutes its fixation has in fact increased in size and relevance to become the definitive universe, the all-that-matters, and, ultimately, the conviction that obsession consciousness, as it spirals down its own funnel towards a point of blistering intensity or into a mania, is genuine enlightenment consciousness, as evidenced especially by its sensational ability to intensify and transfix.

The consciousness of obsession is the home of "I

want ____," "I need," "I crave ____," "I must ____," and that steel I-beamed conviction that security is to be found through the seizing of satiety. It is an orphaned, or partitioned, consciousness which, without guidance or mentoring, has been left to fend for itself, left to its own devices—to life on the street—and its devices, within a world that is perceived as hostile, always spiral around, and gravitate towards, short-term imperatives of gratification, "getting over on," possessing, "nailing down," securing, along with identity altering. Obsession consciousness is the domain of the "hungry ghosts"—those clacking skeletons of repetition and mindless quest that are unaware that they are lacking internal organs with which to digest and utilize what they feel so driven to engage and consume. They are the walking dead.

Indeed, obsession consciousness is the consciousness of consumerism and competitive "upward mobility"—the haven of the sentiment, "He who dies with the most toys (consumption, indulgence or whatever) wins." It is drivenness and fixation at any level of being. "Upward mobility," in the thrall of obsession consciousness, is "downward morbidity."

Obsession consciousness, as it is drawn into ever tighter, more intense spirals of activity, seeks to assert more and more control over its dominion, while managing only to master and bend to the will ever smaller parts of creation. One becomes more and more in control of less and less. The subjective experience of this, however, is at odds with the reality.

Within the encapsulating spell of obsession, one is unaware that the scope of consciousness is shrinking; rather, one perceives that the "size" of consciousness is a volume to be filled, and that the object or focus of obsession consciousness is expanding in volume to fill it. As consciousness implodes, its point of fixation increasingly encompasses, inundates and sucks in everything outside its boundary—including consciousness itself. Obsession consciousness can cannibalize itself.

At the height of its most unseemly, unruly, bully-swagger sway, obsession consciousness is "black-hole" consciousness. If left to its own devices and in no way heeded or offset, obsession consciousness swirls all other conscious intention and motivation across the "event horizon" from which, ultimately, not even a trace of healthy engagement with the world can be extracted.

✦ ✦ ✦

Possession consciousness is subtler, though potentially no less consuming or rapacious. One useful way to approach possession consciousness it to see it as that initially gentle, though persistent, current that carries us along in a direction *in which, at the outset, we quite consciously want to travel.* This "direction" can be the trending towards (or tendency to pursue) any goal, be it personal or professional, regardless of whether such a goal involves the attainment of some kind of standing in life or whether it involves procuring gratifications of any description.

From this very general, broad structural view of possession as "motive force ushering us in a direction," the observation quite naturally follows that we are all possessed. Every life has its tendencies to move in the direction of desire. What is curious about the phenomenology of possession, when considered in this light, is that *possession consciousness, initially, does not typically reveal itself as being operative—that is, it doesn't draw attention to itself as being separate from, or in any way at odds with, personal ego (will-directed) consciousness*. In its ignorance, ego-directed consciousness takes possession consciousness's apparent goals and aims in life as being truly and self-evidently its own.

The awareness—the awakening of ego-consciousness to the reality of its being possessed—to its existing in a state of possession—arises *only* when:

(1) Ego-consciousness decides, for whatever reason, to question the direction in which it is headed.

(2) Ego consciousness concludes, however tentatively—that, indeed, its own goals may actually lie elsewhere than in the direction in which the gently nudging current has been taking it.

(3) Ego consciousness *discovers that it can't get out of the current!*

In fact, it is *just* such an awakening through which ego-consciousness may first even come to identify the existence of the current, having previously only been lulled, unthinking, along by it, entrained in the gentle seduction of the proffered security, perks and assurance it offers.

However, with the discovery of the existence of the current through the questioning of the current's direction and the awakening to one's own unsuccessful personal attempts to change direction by withdrawing oneself from it, the discrepancy between personal goals and "being at the mercy of forces which don't necessarily have my best interests at heart" becomes, at long last, discernible.

And then, perhaps after a number of impulsive, yet concerted and unsuccessful attempts to change direction, with a sinking feeling in the belly, adrenal paralysis in the limbs and a sense of soulful dismay that deflates one's will, one realizes that one is possessed—that one's soul is infested and that one has, by degrees and however unknowingly, willfully given up dominion over oneself—and is now bound to the service of another's beck and call. Something alien—a parasitic hitchhiker, perhaps?... Or, perchance, some unlikely, yet kindred (of kin) consciousness belonging in one's own galactic cluster of consciousnesses, but never before encountered? Whichever it turns out to be, "I" realize that the desire for the goals I have been pursuing, which have historically taken on such a personal aspect as that which "I" really wanted, apparently have their origin, their provenance, elsewhere—and *that* other consciousness (whether alien or related) which promulgates, promotes and pursues these goals is somehow using me and my own life in furtherance of *its* own ends. Oh yes, one little additional item: that "other," it becomes clear, couldn't care less if "I" am destroyed in the process of my enslavement—of being a vehicle through which possession consciousness sates itself on that which it seeks.

Unquestioned, possession consciousness may be lulling me as it lures me towards the wood chipper, presenting it ever in the guise of a gratification (as in an energizing back-scratch). Once questioned, however, possession consciousness is forced to reveal its existence. "I" am *still* headed for the wood chipper (at least initially). But, I now see that it *is* a wood chipper, and I recognize that "I" don't want to be going there, even as I now experience my inability to extricate myself from the current that, unerringly, "trends" me there.

Interesting speculations arise should one attempt to gain entrance into the "mindset" of possession consciousness by personifying it, with the intention of acquiring some comprehension as to its logic and its means. For instance, if I were the consciousness of possession, I realize that the most pervasive perpetration of possession upon another would be accomplished were I *not* to reveal my existence—my identity—as one who possesses, as one who has designs to possess. This hiddenness in which I, as possessor, would realize the foundation of my strength means that I would, as much as possible, be acting from "behind the scenes," unbeknownst to my victim (vehicle). In doing this effectively, I, the possessor, would drop or segue my designs and imperatives into the sluice the possessed's own pattern of wakeful thought or dream-time reverie, and he or she (the possessed) would take these thoughts and intentions as his or her own, never suspecting the locus of their origin lay elsewhere.

Additionally, I—as the possessing consciousness—would be employing another person as a vehicle through which to realize my own ends. These purposes could be anything from using the body of the possessed to embody my own drive to power and influence, or to engage in indulgences of one sort or another (pursuit of sensation(s) and/or emotional intrigue and manipulative subterfuge), or to strive for other objectives that would, in the longer run, likely be quite at odds with the goals, values and possible well-being of the consciousness of the body's customary resident.

I, as possession consciousness, would be looking for a way to manifest bodily, yet still keep my identity—and my very existence—in the background. Presumably, for a person to be a suitable vehicle to "carry me" or "host me," that person would have to have energy on which I could draw, and strong (if acknowledged) desires (on which I could hitch a ride and overlay my own designs), combined with massive "blind spots" in awareness in which I could reside, and from which I could operate, undetected.

Would I, as possessing consciousness, be necessarily aware of the personhood of the person who would be serving as vehicle for me, "hosting" me? Probably not. I would be aware of those aspects of the person which would be capable of hosting and hiding me, and those aspects that could be exploited to my ends, but I would, as possessing consciousness, have no vested interest in the overall health and well-being of my host. As a "silent-partner" parasite, I would only be interested in the person's survival to the extent that he or she—and his or her body—would continue to host me, and be available to do my bidding. If, for any reason, the days for that became numbered, I would have to seek out another hosting situation. Aside from these considerations, the health, wholeness and well-being of my host "vehicle" would likely concern me not at all.

What would make the days "numbered," in which a host might cease to provide a haven and locus of control for possession consciousness? The hint for this lies in the very essence of possession's functioning most successfully from offstage. Because possession consciousness proliferates like a germ culture in damp, dark recesses "behind the scenes," the very surfacing of its existence, and the very acknowledging of its reality in the mind of the person who is being used as vehicle, changes the game, sometimes decisively. Possession consciousness's sphere of existential certainty actually becomes much more hemmed in, and potentially fraught with difficulty, through the host's discovery of its presence.

If I once again venture an attempt to articulate

possession consciousness's view of things upon being discovered, I am tempted to speculate, first, that possession consciousness probably realizes, "Oops, I goofed!" in letting its existence become suspected or known. But as possession consciousness (if such were I) I would not want to be making any concessions, or ceding any territory, or signing over any deeds on my habitation just yet. So I would either have to try to convince my host, by dropping into the background for a while, that, indeed, "I" really don't exist, or I would endeavor to convince my host that she or he is powerless to counter my aims regardless of whether she or he knows about me or not. I could probably count on some leverage for my position due to the host's initial shock, dismay, and sense of hopelessness at discovering the fact of our cohabitation within a single body (and what was assumed to be a unitary mind). Who *ever* wants to make the discovery that one has unwittingly been psychically hosting one or more latch-on hijackers? (No one of my acquaintance.)

If the host can be made to remain deflated and dispirited to a meaningful degree, then possession consciousness's dark, moist abode remains relatively safe. On the other hand, too strong a show of the complete debasement or undermining of the autonomy of the host could lead to suicide—not good for possession consciousness (unless this is its aim, in which case it would already have sized up its next target for psychical infestation).

Yet, for the host, who really has no say in the

matter until the fact of the existence of possession consciousness is recognized, the key is to start to become, as systematically as possible, an *inhospitable*, and ultimately unsuitable, host for possession consciousness. It is to recognize that *possession consciousness's bully swagger and bravado about how powerful it is and how weak its victim is, are actually displays of its own vulnerability to the host—why the need to convince? Becoming an unsuitable host is usually a slow, incremental process in which behavioral integrity and consistency become the constituent factors by which one frees oneself from the tyranny of possession consciousness.*

In such an eventuality, one does not triumph over possession consciousness by vanquishing it through mounting some desperate, direct frontal assault. Such extreme tactics are: (1) usually not sustainable, (2) mobilize in their train the full, situational opposition of possession consciousness, and (3) are likely (sooner rather than later) to collapse under their own weight, reinforcing possession consciousness's assertions of dominance. *Rather, one triumphs by outlasting, and eventually transcending, possession consciousness through becoming a progressively less suitable host for it to such an extent that possession consciousness finally takes leave.* The bodily and psychical abode of the former host has become just too uncomfortable and unpalatable for it.

It may seem quite impossible, when one first has the recognition of being possessed (especially then) to fashion one's release from such a tyranny, and initially the obstacles to freedom are many. Recall that during the earlier blissful times one, clueless as to the actual state of affairs, took possession consciousness's aims as one's own, and in all likelihood fashioned some sort of personal identity, lifestyle and life-structure in which one could reliably take for granted that these aims, however underground or furtive, would be indulged in, and maybe even (at times) sated.

From the standpoint of fashioning one's freedom from possession consciousness, however, all the carefully cultivated particularities of life-structure—which, from the vantage point of unknowingly hosting an indulging possession consciousness, appeared to confer reassurance born of the high degree of predictability that the availability of opportunities to indulge would be ongoing—now become, from the standpoint of extrication, snares and webs still in service to possession consciousness. *Indeed, to fully follow, however incrementally, the promptings of personal autonomy to reestablish mastery and dominion over oneself through becoming an inhospitable host to possession consciousness is to live, in the fullness of time, one's way into a life—and self—transformed.*

So far we have spoken of, and at times personified, possession consciousness as constituting some truly alien force—that is, comprising a sphere of influence that does not ultimately source from, nor belong to, the "possessed person" (the host). The notion of becoming, by way of countermeasure, an inhospitable host to such an assumed alien consciousness—and in so doing, creating conditions in which, eventually, *its* path of less resistance is to depart—actually constitutes a form of exorcism, albeit gradualistic.

What if, however, some of what strikes us as alien, and not sourced with us, really is ours, and belongs with us? This question becomes relevant because much that underlies our conscious orientation is not routinely knowable nor subject to conscious discernment.

In our age the relevance of "unseen forces" has been largely dismissed by the religion of scientism (quantum mechanics, string theory and relativity notwithstanding)—the "age of reason" (and linear causality) run amuck! Whatever it is that does not lend itself to quantifiable observation via the scientific method is deemed as not being at all worthy of study. What a pitiful attitude! Yet what if we really are influenced by innumerable "unseen forces," and, encapsulated in our regimen of daily, deadening routines, are living lives which truncate a fuller experience of who we are—which straight-jacket our own multidimensional nature and the possible magnificence of our own being through a disregard of these forces? *And what if these sides of ourselves fester in frustration at being so disowned and orphaned?*

Could these unacknowledged yet ever-present sides of our nature take on an "alien" aspect in having to resort to whatever it takes to break through into our awareness from such a supine dormancy? *And, if they did present as alien, possessing forces, could their plea be not that they possess us, but that we re-possess them?* Could the destructiveness attributable to truly non-resident aliens as possessing entities also be existent, in some measure, in those surfacing sides of us, as expressions not of their nature and intention, but rather of their woundedness and exasperation about having been so summarily marginalized and rejected by us? In such a circumstance, a "bad actor's," "acting out" would be a cry for attention, and would be indicative of the lengths that a disenfranchised or excommunicated, though ultimately rightful, member of our inner (psychical) family would have to go to gain it.

And what about obsession consciousness? Might this "symptom" not also be, in some instances, the scrawled signature of some despised and cast-off part of us—the note-in-the-bottle which says, "I'm out here (in here) adrift on some trackless ocean. Please send help; come find me. I need to come home."

If what we take as possession by that which holds no rightful place in our inner psychical family is amenable to dislocation via exorcist approaches, then that which rightfully resides within us, however long-forgotten or imposing or scary, should never accede to this approach. Obsession as possession consciousness (indeed, in the Spiritualist movement in nineteenth century America the two terms "obsession" and "possession" were used interchangeably) may be the black hole into which conscious intention is drawn, even as it may be the cry for help through the only still-available means, however primitive (hijacking of the mind—a fitful, desperate clasping of what hasn't yet fallen completely over the edge), through which a cast-off self, living in fright and terror, seeks recognition and a way out, a route home—a means to come in out of the cold and compression of the alien territory where it was cast into exile.

The task then, in such a circumstance, is *not* to exorcise; the task, rather, is to become open, to re-incorporate, to include, to reconcile with, to knowingly coexist with (as necessary), to heal from (if possible), to come into conscious alignment with, to come to terms with (to good purpose, always): to sacrifice a truncated, stunted and entrenched realization of personhood so that a dimensional richness, drawing abundantly on "the unseen," can re-enter. First meetings are likely to be unruly and fraught with challenge—filled with mutual apprehension and suspicion as to motive. However, if initial meetings happen and *no* side of consciousness, including ego-consciousness, gets slaughtered or forced into heavy-handed submission, then fruitful cooperation and collaboration become possible—even from begrudged beginnings. The energy of the cast-off gets re-assimilated as "vitality"; the consciousness of the cast-off receives orientation, and, ultimately, "gains a life," in the four-dimensional space-time existence of the body. From such humble beginnings, in its own time and in full season, may grow coherency and inner bliss.

It is just possible that, amongst humankind, there is no greater adventure within a lifetime than the one just outlined.

The Consciousness of Meditation

Meditation is sampling reality on new wavelengths of perception and cognition. Meditation consciousness is both the awareness that occurs during such times of sampling, and the amalgam of altered awareness and discernment when brought home and *integrated* into all the ongoing moments of everyday life. To comprehend the way in which meditation consciousness arises, it is necessary to start with something closer, and more prosaic, by way of example.

As a kind of thought experiment, let's go back to that field, or patch of urban or suburban lawn (oft visited during our musings on "Vision as the Playground of Consciousness"), and find a spot amidst it in which to sit upright (with something at hand to offer some back support). Once again (I assume that you're not out of practice), in your mind's eye draw a soft gaze on a point of focus and become aware of the canopy of the visual field (roughly the near-hemisphere that was earlier described).

Of course, the area "behind" you—out of your field of view, is (duh!) not visible. So how do we "complete" a sense of the spatial canopy not covered

151

by the visual field? Let's consider hearing.

Hearing also encompasses a field—we might call this the aural, or auditory field. The pinnae of the ears provide a "forward looking" parabola to aural sensitivity, and to that extent hearing tends to favor the direction (i.e., the hemisphere) in which vision is directed—but *only* very approximately. Of course, when visual input issuing from a stimulus and auditory input issuing from a stimulus—the *same* stimulus in this case—are correlated and made coherent by the melding of both wavelengths of perception into a single conjoint experience, these very different perceptual wavelengths are "taken-all-of-a-piece" and assembled into a complete happening, rather than being just a pastiche—the piecemeal pasting together of tatters of different perceptual wavelengths (which, notwithstanding their related origin, they are).

However, in extending the sense of spatial canopy (which surrounds oneself while sitting in this field), beyond what vision (and light) can contribute, it is the wavelengths of sound and the faculty of hearing that supply an impression of the "missing hemisphere."

So when "sound" overlaps "vision," it contributes a deepening tenor of richness to that which is seen (and vice versa). *However, sound is not a "poor cousin" of vision, and its role is not merely to embellish or fill out what is seen.* Indeed, as we have noted, the auditory faculty can, when called upon to do so, penetrate areas and volumes where vision can not (as in the hemisphere of space out of vision's purview).

In fact, sound provides its own sense of spatial canopy, quite independent of vision. In penetrating where vision cannot, it provides its own sampling of unseen realms. Therefore, within its own wavelengths (with their particular capabilities) sound, under certain circumstances, is "superior" to—more effective than—vision. Common examples of this include: the ability of seismic waves (which are much closer to auditory frequencies than to light frequencies) to penetrate, and propagate through, various layers of the earth's mantle (rendering useful information as to the occurrence, location and magnitude of earthquakes anywhere on the earth); the deliberate generation and interpretation of sonic echoes to probe the configuration of geologic strata bearing deposits of oil, gas, or recoverable minerals; and the sonar used for navigation by submarines as they ply the darkened depths of the world's oceans. Sound waves—and seismic waves—can "illumine" these regions, which are closed to light and vision. Of course, the agility of bats on the wing, whether navigating around obstacles or catching a meal in flight, provides evidence that the correct processing of auditory information can give vision a "run for the money." The degree to which this faculty of hearing fine-tunes an organism to its immediate environment—in the "dark," no less—demonstrates a truly remarkable acuity of perception.

So, in our observations and examples regarding the faculties of light and sound, sound both helps to "flesh out" the seen, and *also* samples and assays the unseeable—the "unseen."

This is the analogue to meditation consciousness. Considered as a state, a condition of meditation consciousness largely overlaps, in unexceptional ways, the "known and sampled" universe as we perceive and experience it in our wakeful reality, day in and day out. However, meditation consciousness also extends the range of sampling, perusing and inferring the strata of being beyond the combined range of our everyday sensory experience.

It is the refinement in the discernment of that which arises within periods of meditation that commences to make one aware that a meditative practice, which has usually started with the unremarkable (habitual) ingredients of everyday consciousness and sensation, has started to penetrate, and propagate across, regions of mindscape in ways that extend the range of what is knowable—that start to probe and reveal the existence of an ever-present, yet typically elusive—"unseen" realm of being.

And so there is the "sampling" during meditation. And the wavelengths of sampling (meditation's own) are really extensions of our sensory faculties, those bridging outer and inner—hearing (audition), seeing (vision), touching (tactile), smelling (olfactory), tasting (gustatory), sensing (gestalting)—as well as a small handful of interiorities: intuition ("hunch"-ing), thinking (reflecting), feeling (emoting), and kinesthetic (proprioceptive).

For instance, consider the color "green." Each one of us has his or her own way of experiencing this color while in a relaxed state. A "visualizer"—someone for whom vision is the strong suit for sampling—would "see" green either as a sheet of color or as an object exemplifying that color. However, this is really only one experience of "green." Someone who is primarily auditory would be able to "hear" green; someone with well developed sense of smell would "catch a whiff" of green; someone particularly gifted with taste would, indeed, "taste" some form of it—either registering a taste experienced as directly denoting the color itself, or registering the taste of something specific (a lime, for example)—which incorporates the color as one of its identifying characteristics. Someone tactilely responsive might well "feel" green as a texture of some sort; someone with a keen sense of spatial relationships might "sense" it as a presence (in the absence of any visual experience of the color). Someone else could also have an intuition about green which would constitute the experience of "green" for that person. Ditto "green" thought, "green" emotion, "green" memory, and "green" kinesthetics (postures and holding of the musculature assumed by the body in the name of "green").

Each cognition of "green" would be just as complete—to the person so gifted to perceive along a particular sensory pathway or within a given range of sensory wavelengths—as any other experience of green would be to anyone else who was gifted in another, or other, range(s) of reception.

Who's At Home In Your Body (When You're Not)?

Since most of us have more than one of the sensory faculties and interiorities that are quite well developed, our means of sampling during meditative practice becomes likely to consist of the extension of an amalgam of two or more of our favored channels of perception. This is not at all to say that two or more channels of perception are necessary to meditate. Hardly! Actually, meditative sampling and the development of meditative practice and consciousness need only involve the deepening of any one of the sensory channels, and *one alone is sufficient to develop meditation consciousness in all its richness!*

Therefore, it naturally follows that meditative practice is actually a highly individual—and individualized—activity which, relative to each person, gets developed in accordance with each person's sensory gifts. In short, if you aren't a visualizer (though it can be wonderful if you are), you aren't shut out of meditation consciousness. Sampling can be just as "complete" through any other wavelength. It just takes some practice to discover this to be so.

There are many techniques and approaches to meditation (and each one works for somebody!). There's the "mindfulness" of attending to whatever arises both from within the mind and/or in one's immediate environment (hence the developing of "discernment"); there's "single pointed focus"—whether centered on mantra, the breath, a sound or a visual point[1]—that

---

1) These various (and very different) points of mental focus are suggestive of how meditative practice can develop around any

places a premium on the extinguishing of input outside of "pure mind"; there's an endless array of "visualizing" meditations involving guided imagery, and so on. However, *any good course in meditation will eschew a "one-size-fits-all" approach and, rather, assist would-be practitioners in discovering their own cognitive style for meditating—that is, discovering which sensory channels and techniques are the "strong suits" for each individual meditator*. There are easy exercises for helping each person to open the door to this adventure.

As this little discourse is on meditation consciousness and not on techniques per se, it is time to speak a bit more about the "consciousness" part of meditation consciousness. If meditation consciousness consists of both the "sampling" during meditative practice and the integration of these samplings into our everyday "wakeful" lives, the more imposing and impressive journey is to be found in the realization of the latter rather than the former.

For meditation as a "set aside" experience, in which one "practices" techniques and visits "rarefied" territory or states of mind, becomes an activity (however passive) often set aside from, and held apart from, life in all its messiness in an ongoing present. Don't get me wrong: meditation is beautiful like this, to be sure. One can drop off the world once or twice a day, or in extended sittings over periods of hours, days or weekends (depending on the approach). Oasis med-

---

one (or more) of the senses.

itation, no doubt about it, has its place. I'd be long-since dead without it.

But if we step away from our outer hurly-burly while meditating, what do we bring back from meditation into the hurly-burly besides the feeling that we've "taken a break?" And if we don't bring something more than this back, are we missing out on something? Can rarefied, sublime awareness or moments of ego-identity extinction come back with us across the meditative divide and lend color and hue to who we are—and *how* we are—regardless of outer-world chaos and inner-world unruliness?

The true meditation consciousness, however it is come by, is one in which the discontinuities of consciousness between being "awake, up and about" and "meditating" become more a distinction of degree and less a distinction of kind. This implies the presence of an emotional balance in which the oasis of refreshment has established an ever present co-presence with *us*—has taken up residence within us rather than merely remaining the goal of an activity directed to help us make a get-away to some experience of thing, time or place intentionally set at a distance from us. *Meditation consciousness, then, involves not just visiting a region, but, increasingly, being visited* by *it.*

From the visits to the oasis arise visitations from the oasis to us, wherever we, in our wakeful lives, reside. If the generic, embodied state of meditation is a profoundly relaxed body in concert with a relaxed, yet curiously alert and aware mind, then on our side of the divide the visitations by the oasis lend us more

The Consciousness of Meditation

stress-freed bodies and less plungy, reactive emotions in all our waking hours.

As we continue to probe more deeply into meditative reality, along whatever wavelengths prove useful (and available) to us, sublime discriminations in conscious perception continually evolve on various planes of sampling. The notion of "stepping off the world" gives way, bit by bit, to active, simultaneous presence as felt on all levels of being (mind, body, spirit and heart)—of all ranges of motivation, all possibilities of manifestation. One's being is supported, invisibly yet tangibly, by an infinitude, manifesting here and now as a particularity of energy, identity, form and substance—but *never not having been manifesting in myriad configurations, nor ever to cease manifesting through constant rearrangement and reworked expression.*

What started, within a more limited individual, as a tentative opening and extending to sample new states of "being-connected consciousness," has evolved, within meditation consciousness, into a fresher, expanding realization of being *within* extended consciousness—with these extensions no longer representing journeys or forays only across or out beyond an uncharted frontier, but, rather, now become the current and familiar present outlines of a comfortably enlarged and present self.

Meditation consciousness, then, is the larger "we" who waits, and reaches back, to greet us as we move out from smaller "I" to discover that which breathes us.

As meditation consciousness finds a particular space-time realization within us in the course of becoming a welcomed companion in our daily lives, so we, concurrently, find our own belonging and realization within the infinitude of being as we let it fill us.

We are, and continue to be, our own experiment — and what we most need to discover, and learn about, we become.

Afterword: Intelligence Consciousness

*Our passion takes delight
In measuring from within,
Yet never has it been
Beyond our cosmic plight.*

The Universe is alive with intelligence. Everywhere, at every level, matter, energy and life—all forms of one underlying wisdom—dance their own rhythms in an intertwined destiny. The mind boggles at all that abounds—and is itself one "boggle" of all that abounds. From what is currently observed, each level of creation does what it can to maintain and reinforce the beachhead it has achieved in manifesting at all. There are adaptations and delicate, choreographed balances and fluctuations wherever one peruses, from macro to micro, and along all ranges in between. Each level of intelligence is a mediating consciousness that endeavors to foster survival, correspondence and balance. There is nowhere in this Universe, nor in any range that may be probed, in which this does not seem to be the case. Nature, so to speak, rides all horses.

How do we, as humankind (one mode of intelligence), relate to these countless intelligences that proceed apace, all in, around, through and about us? Scientism, one stripe of human intelligence ever striving for dominion, teases, after a fashion, a number of them, seeking through its own sense of prideful mastery to coerce them to give up their truths to the intelligence of human understanding and sense-making. Human technology, and its cousins, medicine and industry, then takes the fruits of these plucked intelligences and tries to influence, subdue, dominate, channel, digest or apply them in the furtherance of human imperative.

Although each one of the myriad of intelligences, at all levels of being (including the one that enables me to write these words and the one that enables you to read them[1]) proceeds along its own path, for the most part oblivious to the existence of one and all, all these intelligences (including yours and mine) apparently source from within the same "instant" of Big Bang creation, some 13.75 billion years ago.[2,3] Quite possibly

---

1) I'm old fashioned. All my manuscripts are handwritten in their inception.

2) 13.75 billion years presents, at face value, as an inconceivably huge span of time. Yet one way to approach this span in a way that makes it somewhat conceptualizable is to consider that every two years (plus a little) of Earth time, every human being now alive on the planet (6,821,233,320 as of May 15th, 2010 at 10:39 pm, PDT) lives the collective equivalent of 13.75 billion years of human life. In other words, cumulative human life on Earth adds up to approximately 13.75 billion years of human existence — and human consciousness — every two years or so.

3) For some years I have been fascinated by the fact that when

Afterword: Intelligence Consciousness

every thread of every created thing—and every joule of energy that has ever glowed with luminous awakening—was present in that beyond-remarkable point of contact.[4] Most all the multidimensionality of our known and unknown universe, and the apparent separatenesses of a billion-billion things, seems to have precipitated out of this most intimate of origins.[5]

Since so much of "everything" (save, perhaps, for "dark energy," which may be a gravitational effect, sourced in "parallel universes," that feeds through and influences our universe) is sourced within that spectacular Big Bang occurrence, it must follow that most every bit of reality we encounter in our lives is a coincidence—a homecoming that carries within it the

---

research is reported regarding Big Bang theory, reference is made to "this happened within the first 30 seconds of the Big Bang," or "that happened within the first 3 seconds of the Big Bang," and so on. In such statements, it sounds as if there is, so to speak, an outside observer holding a stopwatch, timing the intricate stages of Creation's unfoldment. However, if the dimension of time itself was created (along with all others) within the Big Bang, then how can evidence regarding the Big Bang be calibrated to time as if "time" is linear and a priori—as if it is an independent variable to the Big Bang itself? While a facile-minded physicist may dismiss this question with an offhand remark, I nevertheless have not, to this point, heard this matter raised by lay-readers of physics, nor meaningfully addressed by the professionals.

4) More recent cosmological observations regarding the posited existence of "dark energy" would seem to call into question the extent of the absolute validity of this statement.

5) Our visible universe is estimated to consist of 600 billion galaxies, each of which contains 100 billion stars.

spark of recognition towards whatever we encounter (whether animal, vegetable or mineral, or "energy"), wherever we encounter it, and whenever (since time itself is a "Big Bang" creation) we encounter it. And everything that meets "us" on any level of encounter finds within us the seeds of its own recognition—its own coincidence. *We have never not been intimately connected, in our origins, with everything else.* There is, quite possibly, no part of creation with which, at some prior time, we have not been in intimate relation.

This is one reason—perhaps the largest—why we can feel so "knowing" about people, places, things, ideas, situations, circumstances, institutions, and so on, whom (which) at the level of our day in, day out memory of this specific lifetime, we know we have not specifically "known." In the fullness of creation we have been in intimate contact with every aspect of each and every one of them, right down to levels of the elemental, cellular, molecular, atomic, subatomic, thermal and energetic. Every moment is merely a new arrangement of our own, very ancient, interrelated constituents.

Often, unbeknownst to us, the drive to preserve our individuality is the drive to deny or renounce—to refuse to recognize—the kinship that exists between everyone, and everything, we meet "out there," and all those intrapsychic occurrences, whether delightful or horrendous, that shake loose "in here" (finger pointed at my noggin).

Yes, every moment is a coincidence—we just don't

Afterword: Intelligence Consciousness

recognize it. We are always encountering "lost" — once upon a time known — parts of ourselves. Everything we ever experience, on every level of existence, is a reunion, every heartbeat and inhalation a recognition, a homecoming. In every moment we are already home — there is no place else we can go to, or be.

There are *no* moments of our lives that aren't co-incidences — co-in-ci-den-ces (coincide-nces). Everything we encounter coincides with everything else. Everything we encounter is a re-aquaintance.

Our human consciousness and its intelligence may continue to develop along its own trajectory, but it cannot ever be whole or fulfilled until such occasion as it experiences a reunion (re-union) with — and the unity of — first, its more immediate "cousins," and subsequently, in the fullness of being, all of creation.

Consciousness itself was present at the beginning — maybe even created then — or maybe *was, itself*, the creative demiurge — and, by earth measure, 13.75 billion years of consciousness, more or less, have proceeded since. Perhaps the more conscious reunion that surely awaits somewhere out there, yet to transpire in the infinite possibilities of the enmeshments of time and space (in however many dimensions they may exist), is the fulfillment — the fruition — of the flexations of consciousness that will hold, for the maze of consciousnesses that have developed, evolved and run their course to that point — a moment (I stumble in language by employing a temporal word) of blissful coming together inseparable from a vivid awakening to the reality of kinship—a moment of supreme consciousness and revelation, of sublime enlargement—sufficient as pure cognition—a pure knowing. This integrative moment may be the fulfillment of all consciousness, all intelligences, all destinies. Within such a consciousness lies the epiphany of kinship—now made conscious—between all that is—no longer discernible as "other than"—as anything separate from, or different from—consciousness itself.

Could this be consciousness's greatest realization?

I place my trust in the infinitude of being.

Afterword: Intelligence Consciousness 161

About the Author

Having lived a bi-coastal life for several years, Stephen Rich Merriman now calls Western Massachusetts his home. He takes delight in being amidst family and friends, and living out his roles as husband, father, grandfather, friend and colleague. He seeks to refine his creative output into something worthwhile through pondering the intrinsic worth of any endeavor, including writing, publishing, consulting, composing keyboard music and playing jazz piano.

www.ingramcontent.com/pod-product-compliance
Lightning Source LLC
Chambersburg PA
CBHW031248290426
44109CB00012B/482